HINDU PHILOSOPHY,

THE SANKHYA KARIKA OF
ISWARA KRISHNA

HINDU PHILOSOPHY,

THE SANKHYA KARIKA OF ISWARA KRISHNA.

An Exposition of the System of Kapila.

WITH

AN APPENDIX ON THE NYAYA AND VAISESHIKA SYSTEMS.

BY

JOHN DAVIES, M.A. (CANTAB.)

GYAN

Published by

Gyan Publishing House
5, Ansari Road
Daryaganj, New Delhi-110002
Phone: 011-47034999, 9811692060
E-mail: books@gyanbooks.com

Distribution Network
gyanbooks.com
India, USA, Canada, UK, Australia

ISBN: 978-81-212-5987-3 (PB)
First Published, 1881

2nd Impression 2024

Printed at: Gyan Press, Delhi.

HINDU PHILOSOPHY, THE SANKHYA KARIKA OF ISWARA KRISHNA
Author: JOHN DAVIES

HINDŪ PHILOSOPHY.

THE SĀNKHYA KĀRIKĀ OF ĪŚWARA KṚISHṆA.

An Exposition of the System of Kapila.

WITH

AN APPENDIX ON THE NYĀYA AND VAIŚESHIKA SYSTEMS.

BY

JOHN DAVIES, M.A. (CANTAB.),

MEMBER OF THE ROYAL ASIATIC SOCIETY.

LONDON:

TRÜBNER & CO., LUDGATE HILL.

1881.

PREFACE.

I wish to present to my readers the philosophy of Kapila as it has been set forth by his Indian exponent, Īśwara Kṛishṇa. The system of Kapila, called the Sānkhya or Rationalistic, in its original form, and in its theistic development by Patañjali, contains nearly all that India has produced in the department of pure philosophy. Other systems, though classed as philosophic, are mainly devoted to logic and physical science, or to an exposition of the Vedas.

The system of Kapila may be said to have only an historical value, but on this account alone it is interesting as a chapter in the history of the human mind. It is the earliest attempt on record to give an answer, from reason alone, to the mysterious questions which arise in every thoughtful mind about the origin of the world, the nature and relations of man, and his future destiny. It is interesting, also, and instructive to note how often the human mind moves in a circle. The latest German philosophy, the system of Schopenhauer and Von Hartmann, is mainly a reproduction of the philosophic system of Kapila in its materialistic part, presented in a more elaborate form, but on the same fundamental lines. In this respect the human intellect has gone over the same ground that it occupied more than two thousand years ago, but on a more important question it has taken a step in retreat. Kapila recognised fully the existence of a soul in man, forming indeed his proper nature—the absolute Ego of Fichte—distinct from matter and immortal; but our latest philosophy, both here and in Germany, can see in man only a highly developed physical organisation. "All external things," says Kapila, "were formed that the soul might know itself and be free." "The study of psychology is vain," says Schopenhauer, "for there is no Psyche."

CONTENTS.

NOTES.

Note A.

Note B.

Note C.

Note D.

HINDŪ PHILOSOPHY.

PART I.

THE Hindū schools of philosophy are usually classed in the following order:—

1. The Nyāya, founded by Gautama.
2. The Vaiśeshika, by Kaṇāda.
3. The Sānkhya, by Kapila.
4. The Yoga, by Patanjali.
5. The Mīmāṇsā, by Jaimini.
6. The Vedānta, by Bādarāyaṇa, sometimes called Vyāsa, or Veda Vyāsa.

They are called the six Śāstras, or writings of authority, and sometimes the six Darśanas, views or expositions of doctrine.

The term "philosophy" cannot be strictly applied to all these systems.

The Nyāya is properly a system of logic, offering many points of resemblance to the methods of Aristotle.

The Vaiśeshika treats of physics, of the categories or general attributes of things, and of the formation of the kosmos, which it attributes to the qualities and movements of primitive atoms.

The Mīmāṇsā and Vedānta systems are nearly related to each other.

The Mīmāṇsā, or Pūrva (Prior) Mīmāṇsā, arose from a desire to maintain and illustrate the Vedas. Its object was to support the supreme authority of these books, to maintain their ritual, and to determine the true meaning of such passages as had been misunderstood, or wrested in support of error.

The Vedānta, or Uttara (Posterior) Mīmāṇsā, as it is sometimes called, was formed at a later date on the base of the Upanishads, or treatises relating generally to the Vedas. It differs from the Pūrva Mīmāṇsā chiefly in this, that its main object is to explain and enforce the religious doctrines of the Vedas. It teaches that there is in reality only one existence. It maintains the doctrine of *a-dvaita*, or non-dualism, as decidedly as Schelling or Hegel. All things, visible and invisible, are only forms of the one eternal Essence (τὸ ἕν). The basis of the system is therefore a pure Pantheism. In its later development, this system denied the existence of matter or material forms as objective realities. Visible things are only appearances, a kind of mirage, called *māyā* (illusion).[1]

These systems may be conveniently arranged in three divisions:—

1. The Sānkhya, including the modification of it by Patanjali.

2. The Nyāya, connecting with it the system of Kaṇāda.

[1] Colebrooke's Essays, ii. 400, and note by Professor Cowell.

3. The Mīmāṇsā, both divisions of it being devoted to the support and illustration of the Vedas.

I purpose to treat only of the first of these divisions, adding, as an appendix, an outline of the methods and physical theories of the second.

The Sānkhya Kārikā of Īśwara Kṛishṇa is an exposition of the pure Sānkhya doctrine of Kapila.

OF KAPILA, THE AUTHOR OF THE SĀNKHYA SYSTEM.

THE imagination of the Hindūs has thrown a veil of mystery and fable around Kapila, the traditional author of the Sānkhya philosophy. So much reverence gradually attached to his name, that he was sometimes called "the divine Kapila," and was said to have been a son of Brahmā, the creative form of Brahmă,[1] an incarnation of Vishṇu,[2] or a form of Agni, though born as a son of Vitatha and Devahutī;[3] one of the great ṛishis or ancient sages; a descendant of the great lawgiver Manu; and to have been endowed with knowledge, virtue, freedom from passion, and supernatural power at the time of his birth. We can only say that he was probably a Brāhman, who, being disgusted with the prevailing beliefs and practices of his time, wrought out for himself a system by which he hoped to solve the mysteries connected with spirit and

[1] See Gauḍapāda's Commentary on the S. Kārikā, Wilson's ed., p. 1.; Colebrooke, ii. 242.

[2] "In his (Vishṇu's) fifth manifestation, he (in the form of) Kapila and Lord of Saints, declared to Asuri the Sānkhya (doctrine), which defines the series of principles, and which had been lost through the lapse of time" (Bhāg. Purāṇa, i. 3, 10; Muir, iii. 192; Vishṇu Purāṇa, iii. 2, 18; Bhag. Gītā, x. 26).

[3] In the Bhāg. Purāṇa, however, Kapila is said to have had nine sisters, all born to Kardama by his wife Devahutī (ii. 7, 3; iii. 33, 1).

matter by reason alone. His memory survives only in his system; for of the details of his life or of the time when he lived we have no certain account. It is probable that he lived in the seventh or eighth century before Christ. He is said to have been born at Pushkara, a sacred bathing-place near Ajmeer, and to have dwelt at Ganga Sagar;[1] but there is no reliable evidence in support of either statement. It seems to be certain that he was born in Northern India, and at some time before the birth of the great reformer Gautama Buddha, the date of whose death has been generally assigned to 544 B.C.; for in the Pali Dāṭhavaṁsa, Buddha is said to have been born in the city of Kapila, and that this city, called *Kapila-vastu*, had been built by the sons of Ikshvāku, by the permission of the sage Kapila, and that it was near the Himalaya mountains (i. 20). An indefinite antiquity was sometimes assigned to the system. In the first book of the Mahābhārata, Nārada is said to have taught the thousand sons of Daksha the doctrine of final deliverance (from matter), the surpassing knowledge of the Sānkhya,[2] and he is reckoned as one of the Prajāpatis, or first progenitors of mankind.

Tradition affirms that Kapila lived as a recluse—he is called a *Muni* in Bhag. G., x. l. 52—and that he possessed a supernatural power, not always used with philosophic calmness. In the Rāmāyana (i. 36–44) we are told, with true Oriental exaggeration, that the sixty thousand sons of Sagara, a king of Ayodhyā (Oude), were directed by their father to go in search of a horse

[1] In the Padma Purāṇa he is said to have dwelt in the village of Indraprastha (F. Hall, Introduction to S. Sāra, p. 20).

[2] Ādi-parvan, 3131; Sans. Texts, i. 125.

that had been stolen by a Rākshasa (demon) at an *aśva-medha* (horse-sacrifice). Meeting with Kapila in their search, they accused him of the theft, and the charge so enraged him that he reduced them immediately to ashes.[1]

It does not appear that Kapila separated himself entirely from the Brāhmanic system. It has been said that he "proclaimed the authority of revelation as paramount to reasoning and experience."[2] This, however, is contrary to the main principle of his system, which upholds a knowledge of philosophy as the only way of obtaining the deliverance of the soul from matter. He denies that such a result can be obtained from the Vedas; for they are impure, as ordaining sacrifice, and insufficient for the attainment of this great purpose. He allows "valid testimony" to be one method of proof; and his Vedāntist expounders have interpreted this to be an acknowledgment of the divine origin and authority of the Vedas, but there is no ground for such a statement. The common designation of his system as Nirīś-wara (godless or atheistical) is a sufficient indication that it did not acknowledge a Supreme Lord or a divine revelation. The eminent Vedāntist commentator, Śankara, rightly estimated the position of the Sānkhya system with regard to the Vedas. In his commentary on the Brahma Sūtras he discusses this subject, and concludes: "Hence it is proved that Kapila's system is at variance with the Veda, and with the words of Manu, who follows the Veda, not only in supposing an independent Prakṛiti (Nature), but also in supposing a

[1] Śankara says, however, that it was another Kapila, named also Vāsudeva [a name of Kṛishṇa], who destroyed the sons of Sagara (Commentary on the Brahma Sūtras, ii. 1, 1; Sans. T., iii. 190).

[2] Sanskrit Literature, p. 83.

diversity of souls" (Sans. T., iii. 190). The system of Kapila, if it had been generally adopted, would have been as fatal to the Vedāntist ritual and doctrine as that of Gautama Buddha, which was the natural result or logical issue of the earlier system. In each, knowledge and meditation took the place of religious rites; but Kapila established no society and no hierarchy; he knew nothing of sympathy with mankind in general; he addressed himself to thinkers like himself, and to these alone. Hence his system remained only as a philosophical theory, affecting the whole course of Hindū thought in some respects, chiefly in its physical speculations, but never attaining to a practical supremacy over large masses of men. It was never embodied and crystallised in a concrete form, and as a complete system it has been preserved only as an intellectual product, or as an esoteric doctrine, understood and accepted by a small inner circle of free-thinking men.

It has often been misunderstood. Professor Cousin asserted that it was a pure materialism, though the soul is represented in it as holding a kind of royal supremacy, and all material things are subservient to it. Another writer states, on the contrary, that in this system "souls alone are regarded as substances, whatever affects the soul being ranged under the head of a quality: 1. pleasing; 2. displeasing; or 3. indifferent." The Guṇas, however, are not qualities, but constituent elements, of Prakṛiti, as real in their nature as the soul, and having like it an eternal existence.[1]

[1] The Sānkhya philosophy, whatever may be its merits or demerits, is rarely presented in a correct form by Western writers. Professor Schlüter in describing it says, "Das Selbstbewusstsein (Ahankāra) ist erzeugt und nicht zeugend" (Aristotle's Metaph. eine Toch. de San-

The term *sānkhya* is from the noun *sankhyā*, number, and also calculation, reasoning. In the Mahābhārata it is said: "They (the Sānkhyans) exercise reason (*sankhyā*) and discuss Nature and the twenty-four principles, and are therefore called Sānkhya." Vijnāna Bhikṣhu, in his commentary, explains the noun *sankhyā* as meaning "discrimination," "the setting forth of spirit as distinct from matter (*Prakṛiti*)." Śankara Āchārya gives a similar interpretation (Comm. on the Vishṇu-sāhasra-naman; Introd. to Sānkhya Sāra, by F. Hall). The course of ideas seems to be from number to discrimination, and then to a discriminating judgment, a result of reasoning.

The doctrines of the Sānkhya system have been set forth in many well-known treatises, and on these many commentaries have been written.

1. The *Sānkhya-Pravachana* (Exposition of the Sānkhya), or Sānkhya Sūtras, a work which has been attributed, but erroneously, to Kapila. It appears to be comparatively modern, for it is not mentioned by Śankara Āchārya, who lived probably in the seventh or eighth century A.D.; by Vāchaspati Miśra; or even by the author of the *Sarva-darśana-sangraha*, who is supposed to have lived in the fourteenth century.[1] The most important commentary on this work is the *Sānkhya-pravachana-bhāshya*, by Vijnāna Bhikshu, probably written in the sixteenth century.

2. The *Tattwa-Samāsa*, or Compendium of Principles, a smaller work, also assigned by some, but incorrectly, to Kapila.

khya-Lehre, p. 11). It is, on the contrary, from consciousness, or conscious mind-matter, that the subtle essences of material forms proceed, and from these the gross, visible, manifold forms of sensuous existence.

[1] Introd. to Sānk. Sāra, p. 9.

3. The *Sānkhya-Sāra*, written by Vijnāna Bhikshu. It has been lately edited by Dr. Fitz-Edward Hall, who has prefixed to it a valuable introduction.

4. The *Sānkhya-Kārikā* (Exposition of the Sānkhya), by Īśwara Kṛishṇa. This is a work of high authority on the subject, and appears to be the oldest exposition of Kapila's philosophy that has come down to the present time. An edition of this work was published at Bonn in 1832 by Professor Lassen, with a Latin translation and notes. It was also translated by the late Sir H. T. Colebrooke, and this translation was adopted by Professor Wilson in an edition published by the Oriental Society, to which the commentary of Gauḍapāda, with explanations, was added. It has also been translated into German by Drs. Windischmann and Lorinser, and into French by Messrs. Pautier and St. Hilaire. The latter has added a very extensive commentary.

It consists of seventy-two distichs or ślokas, each expressing in general a distinct principle or dogma. The last three, however, are not connected with the exposition of the Sānkhya system, and are probably a late addition. It is written in the Ārya or Gāthā metre.[1]

It is this work which is now presented to my readers in a new translation with notes, and also occasionally with references to other systems where they coincide with parts of the system of Kapila. It may seem hazardous to attempt the translation of a work which is confessedly obscure and difficult, after the labours of such eminent Sanskrit scholars as Professor Lassen and Sir H. T. Colebrooke; but neither of them has, I think, interpreted the Hindū system, or this exposition of it,

[1] Williams, Sans. Gram., p. 354, 2d ed.

with perfect accuracy. I have had, however, the benefit of their labours, of the occasional remarks of Professor Wilson on Colebrooke's translation, and of the criticism of Dr. Fitz-Edward Hall on Professor Wilson's share of the work. Dr. Hall has criticised some parts of Professor Wilson's work with unnecessary harshness, forgetting that those who follow the footsteps of pioneers in a difficult country may be able to make the path somewhat more distinct than it was before, without possessing as much skill and energy as those who led the way. I have adopted Professor Wilson's translation of Gauḍapāda's commentary, except in a few instances, where I think he has failed to apprehend its right meaning, or the real nature of Kapila's system, which he admits, in his preface, he had not previously studied.

THE SĀNKHYĀ KĀRIKĀ.

By Īśwara Kṛishṇa.

1. "From the injurious effects of the threefold kinds of pain (arises) a desire to know the means of removing it (pain). If, from the visible (means of removing it), this (desire) should seem to be superfluous, it is not so, for these are neither absolutely complete nor abiding."[1]

[1] The first distich is obscure. I subjoin a transliteration of the text (adopting Lassen's reading in the first line, *apaghātakē*, which is found in the S. Tatwa Kaumudī and S. Chandrikā), with the translations of Colebrooke and others :—

du'khatrayābhighātājjijñāsā tadapaghātakē hētau
drishtēsāpārthāchennaikāntātyantato' bhāvāt.

Colebrooke:—"The inquiry is into the means of precluding the three sorts of pain, for pain is embarrassment. Nor is the inquiry superfluous because obvious means of alleviation exist, for absolute and final relief is not thereby accomplished."

Lassen:—"E tergeminorum dolorum impetu (oritur) desiderium cognoscendæ rationis quâ ii depellantur. Quod (cognoscendi desiderium) licet in visibilibus rebus infructuose versetur, non est (infructuosum) propter absentiam absoluti et omni ævo superstitis (remedii)."

St. Hilaire:—"La philosophie consiste à guérir les trois espèces de douleurs. Si l'on pretend qu'il existe des moyens materiels de les guérir, et que, par consequent, la philosophie est inutile, on se trompe, car il n'est pas un seul de ces moyens qui soit absolu ni definitiv."

Fitz-Edward Hall:—"Because of the discomposure *that comes* from threefold pain *there arises* a desire to learn the means of doing away

The first distich gives the chief, if not the sole, purpose of Kapila's philosophy. It is to relieve mankind from the suffering of pain. It is founded on the gloomy view of human life which is generally accepted by Hindū writers. They assert an absolute pessimism. Our present life is not a blessing; it is only a wearisome burden, which is finally cast off when the soul has become free from all contact with matter. The soul then gains, according to Kapila, an absolute independence, a self-existence, which is not affected by any subsequent changes in the outer material world; or it is absorbed, according to the theistic system of Patañjali, into the essence of the One Supreme Being (Brahmă).

The three kinds of pain are explained by the commentators to be—

1. The natural and intrinsic, both bodily and mental (*ādhyātmika*).

2. The natural and extrinsic (*ādhibhautika*).

3. The divine or supernatural (*ādhidaivika*).

The first includes bodily disease and mental infirmity or suffering. The second includes all pain derived from external causes of every kind. The third, as Gauḍapāda interprets it, may be either divine or atmospheric; "in the latter case, it means pain which

therewith *effectually*. If *it be objected, that* visible *means to this end being available*, such *desire* is needless, I demur; for that *these means do* not entirely and for ever *work immunity from discomposure*" (Introd. to S. Sāra, p. 26).

Colebrooke's version of the first part of the distich is not very accurate, and *abhighāta* is not "embarrassment," though Professor Wilson supports this rendering, and censures Lassen for translating it by the Latin *impetus*. It is composed of *abhi* = Gr. ἀμφί, and *han*, for *ghan*, to strike, to slay. In the Peters. Dict. it is explained as *schlag, angriff, beschädigung*. Lassen was confessedly mistaken in his version of the second part. Dr. Hall's is the truest version, but *abhighāta* is much more than "discomposure."

proceeds from cold, heat, wind, rain, thunderbolts, and the like." This, however, belongs to the second division. According to Vāchaspati Miśra, the third kind is "from the influence of the planetary bodies, or by being possessed by impure spirits, such as Yakshas, Rākshasas, &c." But, in old time, the gods of a higher class, and not demons merely, were supposed to afflict men with disease and pain. In the Rig-Veda (ii. 33, 7), Gṛitsamada prays to Rudra that he may be freed from his bodily pains, which he affirms to have been sent by the Devas or gods (*daivya*).[1]

The visible remedies for pain, such as medicine or earthly enjoyments, are not absolute or wholly complete, nor are they eternal; for they do not procure that entire separation of the soul from matter which is an absolute condition of its perfect deliverance from pain.

2. "The revealed (means) are like the visible (*i.e.*, inefficient), for they are connected with impurity, destruction, and excess. A contrary method is better, and this consists in a discriminative knowledge of the Manifested (forms of matter), the Unmanifested (Prakṛiti or primeval matter), and the knowing (Soul)."

By "revelation" the Vedas are meant, which were supposed to have been heard by wise men (*rishis*) as a divine communication, and hence were called Śruti

[1] "O Rudra, who bearest away the disease (rapas) sent by the (other) gods, be gracious, O mighty One! to me." So Apollo sent the plague into the camp of the Greeks (Iliad, i. 42).

(hearing.)[1] In the judgment of Kapila the Vedic system was not perfectly efficient; for (1.) it was impure. It required sacrifice, and thus the blood of animals was shed, often to a great extent. In the Aśwamedha (horse-sacrifice) more than a hundred horses might be sacrificed at one time. According to the Brāhmans, this would avail "to expiate all sin, even the murder of a Brāhman,"[2] and would confer supernatural power; but to Kapila all such rites were impure. (2.) It was connected with destruction. The Vedic system could not give that final exemption from all material conditions without which there must still be a destruction and renewal of bodily life. (3.) It was excessive or unequal, for all men are not wealthy enough to offer costly sacrifices to the gods, and thus the rich man may have more and the poor man less than is due to his individual merit. The Vedas say indeed that there is "no return (to bodily life) for one who has attained to the state of Brahmă;" but in the school of Kapila this blessedness is reserved for those who may attain in the heaven of Brahmā to a discriminating knowledge of soul and matter.[3]

This is the leading principle of Kapila's system. The complete and final blessedness of the soul, which consists of an absolute self-existence, cannot be gained by any religious rites. It is obtained by knowledge, and yet not by every kind of knowledge: it can only be gained by a knowledge of philosophy (which Kapila expounds), and

[1] "By *śruti* is meant the Veda, and by *smṛiti* (tradition, lit. remembrance), the institutes of law (*dharma-śāstra*). These are not to be oppugned by heterodox arguments (contrary to the Mīmāṇsā or Vedāntist exposition), for from them all law or duty (*dharma*) has proceeded" (Manu, ii. 10).

[2] Gauḍapāda's Commentary on this distich.

[3] Sānk. Prav., i. 83, 84; vi. 58.

this treats of existence in three forms—(1.) Manifested or developed matter (*Vyakta*); (2.) the Unmanifested or primal matter, called Prakṛiti or Pradhāna (*Avyakta*);[1] and (3.) the knowing Soul (*Jna*).

This theory of being is unfolded in the following distich and the 22d, which may be brought together for a full exhibition of the system:—

3. "Nature (*Prakṛiti*), the root (of material forms), is not produced. The Great One (*Mahat*= *Buddhi* or Intellect) and the rest (which spring from it) are seven (substances), producing and produced. Sixteen are productions[2] (only). Soul is neither producing nor produced."

Matter in its primal form (*Prakṛiti*) is eternal and self-existing. From it all things emanate, except Soul, which has an independent existence, and is eternal, both *a parte ante* and *a parte post*.

From Prakṛiti proceed: (i.) Intellect (*Mahat* or *Buddhi*), the substance or essence by which the soul obtains a knowledge of external things. It is material,[3] but

[1] In the Institutes of Manu this is an appellation of the Supreme Being. "Then the self-existent Lord, unmanifested (*avyakta*) caused all this universe, with the great principles of being, and the rest, to appear" (i. 6).

Prakṛiti resembles the one universal invisible substance or being of the Platonists, from which all material forms have sprung.

"Διὸ δὴ τὴν τοῦ γεγονότος ὁρατοῦ και πάντως αισθητοῦ μητέρα καὶ υποδοχὴν μήτε γῆν μήτε ἀέρα μήτε πῦρ, μὴτε ὕδως λεγωμεν, μήτε ὅσα ἐκ τούτων μήτε ἐξ ὧν ταῦτα γέγονεν, αλλ' ἀνόρατον εἶδος τι καὶ ἄμορφον πανδεχές" (Timæus, 24).

[2] Properly "modifications" (*vikāra*). They are only developments from a primary form, and have no developing power.

[3] Modern science, like the system of Kapila, makes intellect a mere form of matter. "Mind, used in the sense of substance or essence, and brain, used in the sense of organ of mental function, are at bottom names for the same substance" (Maudsley's Physiology of Mind, 3d ed., p. 38).

of the subtlest form of matter. In the system of Kapila, everything connected in function with sensuous objects is as material as the objects themselves, being equally an emanation from Prakṛiti. The soul exists as a pure inward light,[1] without any instrumentation by which it can become cognisant of the external world. This instrumentation has been supplied, but it is as foreign to the soul, and as objective to it, as any other form of matter.

From Intellect (*Buddhi*) proceeds Consciousness[2] or Egoism (*Ahaṅkāra*); a consequence resembling that of Descartes: "Cogito, ergo sum." Self-consciousness is not, however, in the system of Kapila, a corollary of thought, but inherent in it; or, as Sir W. Hamilton has expressed the same idea, "Consciousness and knowledge each involves the other."[3] It is the same thing in another form, for cause and effect are identical according to Kapila, as water issuing from its source is still the same in reality though not in form. By *Ahaṅkāra* Kapila means a substance or *ens* connected with thought (Buddhi), in which consciousness inheres. It is nearly equivalent to the "mind-stuff" which the late Professor Clifford assumed as the original ground of all being, *i.e.*, of all formal being; a synthesis of mind and grosser matter in which consciousness was produced, by which

[1] Comp. Hegel on Thought (Das Denken), in connection with the Absolute: "Es ist das Licht, welches leuchtet; aber eben keinen andern Inhalt hat, als eben das Licht" (Phil. der Rel., i. 117).

[2] "There are not two worlds, a world of nature and a world of human consciousness, standing over against one another, but one world of nature, whereof human consciousness is an evolution" (Maudsley, p. 57). A dogmatic assertion, but only of a theory, as yet unproved, though offered at first more than 2000 years ago.

[3] Metaphysics, i. 193.

the existence of conscious and unconscious beings was made possible, and was finally developed.

From Ahaṅkāra or Consciousness proceed the five subtle elements (*tanmātra*) which are the primary forms or essences of gross material things, *i.e.*, of all formal life. This might seem to be as pure an idealism as that of Berkeley or Fichte; but there is no idealism in the system of Kapila. Both Consciousness and all existing external forms have a real objective being independent of the soul. In one respect he coincides with the views of Kant, for both agree that we have no knowledge of an external world, except as by the action of our faculties it is represented to the soul,[2] and take as granted the objective reality of our sense-perceptions.[3] In one re-

[1] "There is room for the supposition that even the ultimate particles of matter may be permeable to the causes of attractions of various kinds, especially if those causes are immaterial; nor is there anything in the unprejudiced study of physical philosophy that can induce us to doubt the existence of immaterial substances; on the contrary, we see analogies which lead us almost directly to such an opinion. The electrical fluid is supposed to be essentially different from common matter; the general medium of light and heat, according to some, or the principle of caloric, according to others, is equally distinct from it" (Dr. Thomas Young, Unseen Universe, p. 160). The authors of this work would substitute "not grossly material" for "immaterial," and "gross matter" for "matter" in the passage quoted. They correspond to the *tanmātra* and *mahābhūta* of Kapila.

[2] "Bedenkt man dass diese Natur an sich nichts als ein Inbegriff von Erscheinungen, mithin kein Ding an sich, sondern blos eine Menge von Vorstellungen des Gemüth's sei, so wird man sich nicht wundern sie blos in dem Radicalvermögen aller unser Erkenntniss, nämlich der der transcendentalen Apperception in derjenigen Einheit zu sehen, um deren Willen allein sie Object aller möglichen Erfahrung, d. i. Natur heissen kann" (Kant, Deduction of the Categories, p. 576).

"After all, what do we know of this terrible 'matter,' except as a name for the unknown and hypothetical cause of states of our own consciousness" (Huxley, Lay Sermons, p. 142).

[3] Cf. the Sāṅkhya Sāra (i. 41, 42). The Vedāntist objects that "since nothing exists except thought, neither does bondage, for it has no cause." The reply is, "Not thought alone exists, because there is the intuition

spect there seems to be in the Hindū theory a germ of the system of Hegel, in which subject and object are made one by an absolute synthesis; for the substratum of thought and consciousness and of the external world is the same in kind, since elementary substances issue from consciousness, and consciousness proceeds from intellect (*Buddhi*). There would be some resemblance if the system of Kapila ended with Nature (*Prakṛiti*). But there is still a dualism. The soul is different in kind from all material things, and will finally be severed from them by an eternal separation. When finally separated from matter, including intellect and all the forms or emanations of Prakṛiti, it will have no object, and no function, of thought. It will remain self-existent and isolated in a state of passive and eternal repose.

To the five subtle principles are given the technical names of *sound, tangibleness* or *touch, odour, visibility* or *form*, and *taste.*

From these primary essences proceed the five gross elements (*mahābhūta*). These are: (1.) *ether* (*ākāśa*), from the subtle element called *sound;* this fills all space and envelops all things; (2.) *air* (*vāyu*), from the element *tangibleness;* (3.) *earth*, from the element *odour;* (4.) *light* or *fire*, from the element *visibility;* and (5.) *water*, from the element called *taste.*

of the external." The objector replies, "From the example of intuitive perception in dreams, we find this (your supposed evidence of objective reality) to exist even in the absence of objects." The rejoinder is, "Then if one does not exist, the other does not exist, and there is only a void;" "for," the commentator, Vijnāna Bhikshu, adds, "if the external does not exist, then thought does not exist. It is intuition that proves the objective, and if the intuition of the external does not establish the objective, then the intuition of thought cannot establish it (thought)."

From Consciousness proceed also (6.) the five organs of sense (*indriya*),[1] which are the eye, the ear, the nose, the tongue, and the skin; and (7.) the five organs of action; the voice, the hands, the feet, the anus, and the organs of generation. Lastly, it produces the *manas*,[2] which is the receptive and discriminating faculty. It receives and individualises the impressions made by outward objects on the senses. These it submits to Consciousness, by which an attribute of personality is given to them, and through which they pass on to the Intellect (*Buddhi*). By this last faculty the sense-perceptions are defined and represented in a full, distinct form. The soul beholds these presentations as objects are seen in a mirror, and thus has a knowledge of the external world.

(ii.) The next object of inquiry (the first in point of existence) is the primal source of these material existences, or the Unmanifested (*Avyakta*).[3] This is the primordial matter, from which all material things have emanated or

[1] Kapila saw that consciousness was the base of the reality of all our sense-perceptions. "Soll Etwas überhaupt etwas Reelles im Gegensatz gegen das blos Eingebildete bezeichnen, so mus das Ich wohl etwas Reelles sein, da es *Princip* aller Realität ist" (Schelling, System des Transcen. Idealismus, p. 60).

"Both sensation and reflection are thus original states of consciousness, and exist only in so far as we are conscious of them. For example, I see and I am conscious that I see. These two assertions, logically distinct, are really one and inseparable. Sight is a state of consciousness, and I see only in so far as I am conscious of seeing" (Dean Mansel's Letters, Lectures, &c., p. 162).

[2] "There exists, latent or potential, in the sensory centres, something that may be called a faculty, which on the occasion of the appropriate impression, renders the sensation clear and definite; in other words, gives the interpretation" (Maudsley, p. 237). This is the *manas* of Kapila.

[3] "Here let us remind our readers of the argument by which we were led to conclude that the visible system (the *Vyakta* of Kapila) is not the whole universe, . . . and that there must be an invisible order of things (*Avyakta*), which will

have been evolved. It is eternal, universal, single, *i.e.*, without parts, invisible, and is inferred only by reasoning from present, actual existences, which must have a cause. It is not produced, but is productive, having within itself the potentiality of all being, except soul. The Vedāntists incorporated it in their system, making it the Brahmī, or productive energy, of Brahmā.

(iii.) The soul, which is uncompounded and eternal, neither a product nor producing. The system of Kapila only recognises each individual soul, but the theistic Sānkhya asserts the existence of a supreme soul, the Lord (*Iśwara*) of all, the intelligent cause of the emanations from *Prakṛiti* (Nature).

These form the twenty-five principles, or categories of being, laid down in the Sānkhya system. They are the base of nearly all the philosophy of India.

In the following distichs the methods by which all true knowledge is obtained are determined, according to the judgment of Kapila.

4. "Perception, inference, and fit testimony are the threefold (kinds of) accepted proof, because in them every mode of proof is fully contained. The complete determination or perfect knowledge (*siddhi*) of what is to be determined is by proof."[1]

remain and possess energy when the present system has passed away. . . . It is, moreover, very closely connected with the present system, inasmuch as this may be looked upon as having come into being through its means" (The Unseen Universe, p. 157; see also p. 158).

[1] Colebrooke's translation is, "It is from proof that *belief* of that which is to be proven results," and this version is supported by Professor Wilson, on the ground that the Hindū commentators explain the word *siddhi* (accomplishment, perfect knowledge) by *pratīti*, "trust," "belief;" but in the Petersburg Dictionary this is explained as

5. "Perception is the application[1] (of the senses) to special objects of sense. Three kinds of inference are declared: it (an inference or logical conclusion) is preceded by a *liṅga* (mark or sign = major premiss) and a *liṅgī* (the subject in which it inheres = minor premiss). Fit testimony is fit revelation (*śruti*)."

6. "The knowledge of formal or generic existence is by perception; of things beyond the senses by inference; that which cannot be determined by this (method) and cannot be perceived must be determined by fitting means."[2]

Perception results from the action of any of the organs of sense on its proper objects.

Inference (*anumāna*) is the process of reasoning. The conclusion that is drawn from it is *anumiti* (Tarka Sangraha, p. 30).

The Nyāya or Logical school admits four kinds of

meaning: (1.) a drawing near (hinzutreten, nahen); (2.) a clear insight into a matter, a full knowledge, conviction (klare Einsicht in Etwas, volkommenes Verständniss, Ueberzeugung). Lassen's translation is, "Nimirum demonstrandæ rei consummatio (oritur) e demonstratione," adding in his commentary, "Ultimam sententiam ita accipio ut dicatur id quod demonstrandum sit, magis minusve absoluta evidentia posse evinci secundum genus demonstrationis qua probetur." Proof, however, is here spoken of absolutely. There is no question of degree.

[1] *Adhyavasāya*, a word difficult of explanation. Colebrooke translates it by "ascertainment," Lassen by "intentio (sensuum)," St. Hilaire by "application." In the Amera Kosha it is glossed by *utsāha* (force, effort, application). The authors of the Petersburg Dictionary only quote from Hindū commentators some untranslated glosses, adding that some explain it as meaning "a strong will or effort."

[2] *Āptāgamāt*, from "revelation" (Colebrooke); "revelatione" (Lassen); "par une information legitime" (St. Hilaire).

proof: (1.) *pratyaksha* (perception); (2.) *anumāna* (inference); (3.) *upamāna* (comparison or analogy); and (4.) *śabda* (verbal testimony). To these the Vedāntic school adds *arthāpatti* (presumption), an informal kind of inference; as, "Devadatta does not eat by day and yet is fat, it is presumed therefore that he eats by night;" and *abhāva* (non-existence), a method of proof from an impossibility, or a *reductio ad absurdum*, as, "There can be no flowers in the sky."

By the latter part of Distich 4, Kapila limits all possible knowledge to his three methods of proof. He rejects all innate ideas, and all knowledge derived from pure consciousness. He does not admit any moral sense as inherent in the soul. This only knows or sees what *Buddhi* (intellect) presents to it. He adopts the axiom, "Nihil est in intellectu quod non prius in sensu;" and as neither sensation nor intellect can present the form of an eternal self-existent Author of all things, the doctrine of a Supreme Deity was not admitted into his philosophy. Kant has contended that the idea of God cannot be derived from reason, but only from the facts of our moral consciousness, which have no place in Kapila's system. Goodness or virtue is an attribute of *Buddhi*, which is only a form of matter. The soul has no concern with it. The only real evil is pain, and this can only be destroyed by an eternal separation of the soul from matter, which is obtained by knowledge, not by moral or religious virtue.

There is the same obscurity in the language of Distich 5 as in our use of the word "perception;" for *dṛishṭam* (thing seen) properly denotes not the application of the eye to objects of sense, but the result of that process. The use of the term "application" is, however, strictly in accordance with the Hindū theory of the method of perception. The knowledge gained by the eye is not from rays of light proceeding from an object, but by a ray of light proceeding from the eye.

An inference, according to the Nyāya school, is "knowledge produced from a logical antecedent.[1] This consists in the knowledge of a general principle combined with the knowledge that the case in question is one to which it is applicable." In the Nyāya Sūtra Vritti inference is said to be threefold: (1.) "*Prior,* that is, cause, characterised by or having that (cause); as inference of rain from the gathering of clouds; (2.) *posterior,* effect characterised by it; as inference of rain from the swelling of a river; *analogous* or *generic,* characterised as distinct from both effect and cause; as the inference of anything being a substance from its being earthy." This is reasoning *a priori,* from cause to effect; *a posteriori,* from effect to cause; and by *analogy,* or community of properties.

The terms *liṅga* (character or mark) and *liṅgī* (the subject of the *liṅga*) answer nearly to the major and minor premisses of Western logicians. In the syllogism, commonly given as an example—

> "Whatever smokes has fire;
> This hill smokes;
> *Ergo,* This hill has fire,"[2]

[1] Tarka Sangraha, p. 29. The word *parāmarśa,* translated "logical antecedent" by Ballantyne, is translated by Wilson "observation," "experience;" prim. taking hold and then apprehension by the mind. In logic it means a fact or truth apprehended by observation. "For example, the knowledge that this hill is marked by smoke, which is always attended by fire, is a *parāmarśa.*"

[2] In the Tarka Sangraha (p. 32), the knowledge that this "mountain is characterised by smoke (the *liṅga*), which is invariably attended by fire," is called a *liṅga parāmarśa,* which means "such recognition of a sign as leads to inference."

the first proposition contains the *liṅga*, which here is smoke, and the second the *liṅgī*, or that in which the *liṅga* inheres. By "revelation" is meant either the teaching of the Vedas or of other works supposed to have a similar or equal authority. Kapila, who was doubtless a Brahman, did not wholly reject the Vedas, but he treats them with little respect, and makes their authority subordinate to that of reason. His Vedāntist commentators draw conclusions from this passage which are inconsistent with the first and second distichs, which express Kapila's fundamental principle.

By "formal or generic existence" in Distich 6 (*sāmānya*[1]) is meant all the related forms or genera of the material world. In the Tarka Sangraha (p. 56) it is thus explained: "Community (*sāmānya*) is eternal, one, belonging to more than one, residing in substance, quality, and action. It is of two kinds, the highest and what is lower. The highest is existence (*sattwa*, primal matter ?); the lower is genus (*jāti*, family or race), such as have the nature of substance (elementary substance), and the rest."[2] It is used in the latter sense in the passage which we are now considering.

[1] In the Sānkhya Bhāshya it is maintained that *sāmānya* here means "analogy," and that *dṛishṭāt* is put in apposition with *anumānāt*. The passage must then be translated, "The knowledge of things beyond the senses is obtained by inference, *i.e.*, by the perception of analogy." Wilson and St. Hilaire adopt this view, but it is opposed by the following considerations:—(1.) The word *sāmānya* is not used by Hindū logicians to denote analogy, but a generic form of being; (2.) reasoning by analogy, or a perception of it, is not equivalent to the whole of the inferential process, but only a part of it. I adopt, therefore, the conclusions of Colebrooke and Lassen; but Colebrooke's translation of *sāmānya* by "sensible things," and Lassen's by "æqualitas," do not represent with sufficient exactness its meaning.

[2] *Dravyatwa*, having the nature of substance, from *dravya*, substance, which sometimes means elementary substance, as fire, earth, &c. See Burnouf, *s. v.*

Things beyond the senses are not only those which are too subtle for the organs of sense, but those which are imperceptible by accident, as the fire in a mountain that smokes.

Whatever lies beyond perceived or inferred existence can only be known by testimony.

7. "(This want of perception may be) from excessive distance, too great nearness, destruction of organs, inattention of the mind (*manas*), minuteness, concealment (by other objects), predominance (of other things), and by intermixture with like objects."

8. "From the subtlety (of Nature), not from its non-existence, it is not apprehended (by the senses); it is apprehended (or perceived) by its effects. Intellect (*Buddhi*) and the rest (of the derived principles) are its effects, which have an unlike and a like[1] form to Prakṛiti (Nature)."

9. "Existing things (*sat*) are (proved to be) effects from the non-existence of (formal) being by the non-existence of cause; by the taking (by men) of a material cause (to produce anything); from the non-existence of universal production (by every cause); from the possible causality of an efficient agent (only); and from the nature of cause."

[1] Lassen has in the text *swarūpam* (having its own form), from the Sānkhya Kaumūdi, which must be referred to intellect (Mahat). All the MSS. but one have *sarupam* (like), which the sense requires. In his translation he has "dissimile et simile."

Kapila, or his expounder, contends in Distich 6, as the philosophers of the Eleatic school, against the assumption that the senses are the only sources of knowledge. Our senses are limited in their own nature, and their action is imperfect from many opposing circumstances. Hence many things exist which they cannot reveal, and they give imperfect information of things which lie within their range. The intellect (*Buddhi*) must arrange and present our sense-conceptions, that there may be a true cognition. In this way we rise from the knowledge of the manifold to the conception of the one, in which all things were contained and from which they have issued. Kapila, however, confines this oneness to primordial matter, *Prakṛiti*. He does not refer the existence of souls to one supreme spiritual Being, as the theistic school of Patanjali.[1] Herein he differs, too, from the Vedāntists, who maintain that all things are the one supreme Spirit; that the visible things of the outer world are only *māyā* (illusion), the deceptive form with which the Invisible is veiled; and that, therefore, there is neither cause nor effect: all things inhere in, and indeed are, the One sole Existence.

But the world, as it exists, was to Kapila an effect.

[1] Dr. Fitz-Edward Hall says that "alike in both the Sānkhyas there is acknowledgment of a being superior to the gods. He is made up of an immaterial part, *purusha*, or 'person,' and of an *anta'karaṇa* or 'internal organ,' which is Prakṛiti (Nature)" (Introd. Sānk. Sāra, p. 2). This statement is not supported by anything in the Sānk. Kārikā, and in the Sānk. Pravachana it is expressly stated that "they (the Vedas) are not the work of Purusha, from the non-existence of a Purusha (purushasyābhāvāt). Vijnāna Bhikshu adds, "Supply, because we deny that there is a Lord" (v. 46). Some of the followers of this school asserted the existence of a personified sum of existence, called Hiraṇya-Garbha (Professor Cowell, Note in Elph. India, p. 126); but Kapila did not recognise such a being. His Prakṛiti is impersonal matter.

He proceeds in Distich 9 to prove this proposition by arguments which have received very different interpretations. Colebrooke translates the first part of the distich thus: "Effect subsists (antecedently to the operation of cause), for what exists not can by no operation of cause be brought into existence." The doctrine of Kapila is indeed that cause and effect are so far identical that an effect is only a developed cause, but this part of his argument is contained in the sixth clause of the distich, where he argues from the nature of cause. The general argument or the main proposition to be proved is, that formal existence *is* an effect, implying a cause, not that effect exists antecedently in its cause. Professor Wilson adopts Colebrooke's translation, and explains the passage as if in accordance with this view, but in reality he confounds two distinct ideas. "It is laid down," he says, "as a general principle that cause and effect are in all cases co-existent, or that effect exists anteriorly to its manifestation: *sat-kāryam*, in the text, meaning existent effect prior to the exercise of the (efficient) cause; or, as the phrase also of the text, *asadakaraṇāt*, is explained, 'If effect prior to the exercise of (efficient) cause does not exist, its existence cannot by any means be effected.' The expression *sat-kāryam*, therefore, is to be understood throughout as meaning 'existent effect,' not the effect of that which exists, and the object of the stanza is to establish the existence of cause from its effects, and not of effects from the existence of cause, as Professor Lassen has explained it: 'Quænam sint rationes docetur quibus evincatur mentem ceteraque principia effecta esse a τῳ ὄντι.'" Here the two propositions, that effect exists *in* its cause, and that formal existence is an "existent effect," are confounded, and the last part of the sentence is not in harmony with the statement of the proposition as laid down in the beginning. The words *sat-kāryam* express the proposition to be proved, which is that *sat*, manifest or formal existence, must be considered as wrought; or, in other words, is an effect implying an efficient cause. The phrase does not mean "an existent effect," but that what *is* formally existent is necessarily an effect. Causality is implied as an absolute condition of all formal being. *Asadakaraṇāt* (literally from non-existence, non-cause) implies that there is an identity in the terms non-existence and non-cause, and that we cannot conceive of formal existence as uncaused: only the unformed *Prakṛiti* (Nature) is without a cause, having existed eternally. (See p. 17.)

Lassen translates the first argument thus: "E nulla non entis efficacitate . . . colligitur illum effectum esse effectum τοῦ ὄντος." Professor Wilson remarks, "It is here to be objected that the *ens* (*sat*) is the result, not the agent;" but Lassen here means by the τὸ ὄν, not any simple or formal existence, but the unformed *Prakṛiti*, which is the true material cause of the whole series of existent things. The argument implies that the idea of cause is involved in the idea of formal existence, and that we can only conceive of any limited conditioned life as produced by something that preceded it, which is as truly existent as the effect, until we come to what is formless and unconditioned, *i.e.*, Prakṛiti (Nature).

M. Cousin has entirely mistaken the meaning of Kapila's argument. He understands it as really denying the existence of cause, because cause and effect are, in the system of Kapila, of the same nature. "Selon Kapila il n'y a pas de notion propre de cause, et ce que nous appelons une cause n'est qu'une cause apparente relativement à l'effet qui la suit, mais c'est aussi un effet par la même raison, et toujours de même, de manière que tout est un enchaînement nécessaire d'effets sans cause véritable et independente." It is difficult to imagine how such a theory could be attributed to Kapila after reading any of the well-known expositions of his philosophy. Any link in the series of existent things may be a cause of that which follows and an effect of that which has preceded it; and hence, as Kapila argues, we must admit a primal material cause, itself uncaused, from which all existent things have ultimately proceeded. He did not admit a supreme *spiritual* Being, an *Īśwara* or Lord, either as the Author or Ruler of the visible world, but he argued for the existence of a primal *material* cause (*Prakṛiti*) as the necessary antecedent of every other existence.

M. St. Hilaire translates the clause as follows: "Ce qui prouve bien que l'effet provient de l'être, c'est que le non-être ne peut être cause de quoi que ce soit;" but this makes Kapila *assume* that the existing world is an effect springing from a cause, but his proposition is to prove that it *is* an effect, and that therefore there must have been a primary cause. His standpoint is existence in the manifold conditioned forms of things as they are, and that such forms must have had a primary cause, *i.e.*, that they are effects. The *nature* of cause forms the last clause of the distich. He rises finally at the end of the series, traced in an ascending line, at a true cause, which is, however, identified in kind with the effects which have issued from it.

Mr. Mill's definition of cause is more clearly expressed,

but is insufficient: "It is an universal truth," he says, "that every fact which has a beginning has a cause," and "an invariability of succession is found by observation to obtain between every *fact in nature* [which Kapila calls *sat*] and some other fact which preceded it."[1] So cause is defined, but more precisely, in the Tarka Sangraha: "That which invariably precedes an effect *that cannot else be* is a cause." It is this law of *succession* which Kapila declares to be invariable and necessary as to all the facts or formal existences in Nature.

In the second clause he appeals to the common observation of mankind that cause and effect mutually imply each other. If you wish to produce anything, you must use means for the accomplishment of your end. This cause must also bear a relation to the effect; it must be of the same nature, as stated in the third clause. If

[1] Mill's theory of causation (which is that of Dr. Thomas Brown), that it means only the idea of an invariable sequence, is insufficient, for we cannot think of cause without conceiving a necessary and invariable power inherent in it by which the effect is produced. The definition in the Tarka Sangraha is more precise. It declares the necessity of a cause in relation to an effect. But the idea of power is not distinctly enunciated by either. It is well expressed by the late Professor Wilson: "We do not fear to say that when we speak of a power in one substance to produce a change in another, and of a susceptibility of such change in that other, we express more than our belief that the change has taken and will take place. . . . There is, besides this, the conception included of a fixed constitution of their nature which determines the event—a constitution which, while it lasts, makes the event a necessary consequence" (Quot. in Hamilton's Metaph., ii. 383, 384). "It is a self-evident maxim that every event must have a cause. After contemplating an event in life or nature, I find myself going in thought beyond it to consider how it came to pass; by some instinctive law, some constitutional motion inherent in my mind, I go in the direction of a cause for that event; something not merely antecedent to it, but which stands in such a relation to it as that, in consequence of it, that event or thing exists" (Professor Mozley's Essays, The Principle of Causation, i. 416). See Sir W. Hamilton's Discussions in Philosophy, App. I.

you would have cheese, you must use milk and not water; for one cause is not equal to the production of every effect. An efficient cause is also necessary for the production of an effect as well as a material cause. A potter is necessary for the making of a jar; he is not competent to produce cloth.

The last argument of Kapila is "from the *nature* of cause," or, as Vāchaspati explains it, "the identity of cause and effect."[1] This would have been more properly placed at the beginning of the distich, for it shows what he meant by *cause*, which he explains as a material source from which an effect issues. As oil is extracted from sesamum seeds, we have in the latter the material cause or source of the oil which was in the seeds before it was extracted by pressure. His idea of cause and effect is of an antecedent form or substance, of which the effect is an emanation.[2] Effect is a developed cause and cause is an undeveloped effect; both are the same in substance, and

[1] Sir W. Hamilton also declares the identity of cause and effect, so far as that an effect must have previously existed in the cause. "What is the law of causality? Simply this: . . . That all that we at present come to know as an effect must have previously existed in its causes" (Metaph., ii. 400). Not absolutely so, for the effect may differ, and, in truth, must always differ, in some respect from the cause.

[2] So, according to Aristotle, the ancient Greek philosophers taught: "Τούτων δὲ τὸ μὲν ἐκ μὴ ὄντων γίνεσθαι ἀδυνατον· περὶ γαρ ταύτης ὁμογνωμόνουσι τῆς δόξης ἅπαντες οἱ περὶ φυσεως" (Phys., i. 4). Mr. G. H. Lewes goes further than Kapila, for he practically denies that there is any difference between cause and effect. "I have endeavoured to show that the supposed axiom of causes not being knowable when their effects are known is a fallacy and a misapprehension of the principle of causation; it is plausible only through the metaphysical postulate that the cause is something different from its effects" (Fort. Rev., April 1876). Kapila taught that the effect must be of the same *kind* as the cause, but he also taught that one may differ from the other in many ways. The potter (instrumental cause) and the clay (material cause) are not the same as the jar produced.

hence, from the nature of cause, it involves the effect in itself, as that which is evolved implies the cause or material source from which it has been evolved. Now all formal life is a development, and implies that from which it has been developed. It seems, however, to be forgotten that the *efficient* cause, as the potter in making a jar, is something altogether different from the clay with which he works and the jar which he produces.

The nature of visible or developed things is then discussed, in contrast with the invisible or undeveloped source (*Avyakta*), which is Prakṛiti.

10. "That which is visible or developed has a cause; it is not eternal or universal; it is mobile (modifiable), multiform, dependent, attributive, conjunct, and subordinate. The undeveloped principle is the reverse."

The visible or developed universe contains the twenty-three principles (*tattwa*, existence, reality), which are emanations from *Prakṛiti* (Nature).

It is caused, for it proceeds from Prakṛiti; it is therefore not eternal as manifestation or form, but is eternal as being one with its source; for "destruction," says Kapila, "is a return to the producing cause."

It is not universal or pervading (*vyāpi*): each of these principles (*tattwa*) is not found in every form.

It is mobile, admitting changes of position in different bodies.

It is multiform, existing in various forms of aggregation.

It is dependent or conditioned;[1] each of the grosser elements is dependent upon the more subtle, and these are dependent on consciousness, &c., up to Prakṛiti.

It is attributive or predicative (*liṅgam* [2]), *i.e.*, each substance has a characteristic sign or quality which may be predicated of it.

It is conjunct or conjunctible, for the elements combine with one another.

It is subordinate or governed, each being subordinate to the other in an ascending series, up to Buddhi (intellect).

Prakṛiti, however, is uncaused, eternal, universal, self-existing, and supreme.

11. "The manifested (*Vyakta*) has the three modes (*guṇa*). It is indiscriminating, objective, generic,[3] irrational,[4] and productive. So also is *Pradhāna* (Nature). Soul in these respects, as in those (previously mentioned), is the reverse."

12. "The modes have a joyous, grievous, and stupefying nature. They serve for manifestation, activity, and restraint: they mutually subdue and

[1] *Āśritam.* Lassen translates it by "innixum;" Colebrooke by "supporting;" St. Hilaire by "accidentel." The Petersburg Dict. has "Halt und Schutz bei Jmd suchend," lit. "going to one" (for protection or support).

[2] *Liṅgam.* Colebrooke translates it "mergent," *i.e.*, subject to dissolution, after Gauḍapāda; but Professor Wilson remarks that "predicative" or "characteristic" would be a preferable translation. Lassen has "reciprocans," but he adds "dubiæ mihi est significationis." See the Tarka Sangraha, p. 38 (Ballantyne).

[3] *Sāmānyam*, translated by Lassen and Colebrooke "common." See p. 26.

[4] *Achetanam*, from *a*, neg. part, and *chit*, to perceive, to know.

support each other, produce each other, consort together, and take each other's condition."[1]

13. "'Goodness' (*sattwa*) is considered as light (or subtle), and enlightening (or manifesting); 'passion' or 'foulness' as exciting and mobile; 'darkness' as heavy and enveloping (or obstructive, *varaṇaka*). Their action, for the gaining of an end, is like that of a lamp."[2]

These distichs introduce an element in the Sānkhya philosophy which plays an important part in its physical and moral teaching. It is that of the three *guṇas*, or qualities, as the word is generally translated. They are not qualities, however, but the constituent elements of Nature (*Prakṛiti*). "These three qualities," says Colebrooke, "are not mere accidents of Nature, but are of its essence and enter into its composition." Nature, or primordial matter, is described in the system of Kapila as formed by the *guṇas*, which were primarily in equili-

[1] *Vṛittayas.* Vāchaspati interprets the word by *kriyā* (act, operation), and connects it with each of the foregoing terms (Wilson, p. 51). The Sānk. Bhāshya interprets this part by "parasparam varttante" (are reciprocally present). St. Hilaire has "se suppléent reciproquement." *Vṛitti* means state, condition, or manner of being, and the meaning is that each *guṇa* may, in some circumstances, assume the nature of the others, or be the same in effect. See p. 26.

[2] *Sattwa* (goodness or reality), *rajas* (passion), and *tamas* (darkness) are the usual names of the three *guṇas*. In the preceding distich they are named from "*prīti*" (joy or love), *aprīti* (aversion), and *vishāda* (stupefaction or dulness). The first is said to include rectitude, gentleness, modesty, faith, patience, clemency, and wisdom; the second produces hatred, violence, envy, abuse, and wickedness; and the last causes tardiness, fear, infidelity, dishonesty, avarice, and ignorance (S. Chandrikā, Wilson, p. 52).

brium, and so long as this state existed there was no emanation into separate forms of matter. This state of rest was destroyed when Nature began to act, though unconsciously, for the welfare of soul,[1] and this movement, as motion or activity in general, is due to the influence of that *guṇa*, or constituent of Nature, which is called "passion" (*rajas*). This theory seems to be contrary to a previous statement that Nature is one; but it is conceived as we apprehend light to be a simple colourless substance, though formed by a perfect union of the coloured rays, whose individuality is lost or undeveloped in that which we call light.

The *Guṇas* are a mere hypothesis, invented to account for the manifest differences in the conditions of formal existences. There is evidently a subtle or spiritual element, one of passion or force, and something which is contrary to both, an element of dulness or insensibility, in at least all human beings;[2] and these are assumed by Kapila to indicate a primary difference in the constituent elements of Nature (*Prakṛiti*). The same idea seems to have presented itself to some of the earlier Greek philosophers, as Aristotle has described their doctrine.[3]

[1] "The governorship thereof (of soul over Nature) is from its proximity, as in the case of the gem" (Sānk. Sāra, i. 96). The interpretation is, "that as the gem (the loadstone) is attracted by iron merely by proximity, without resolving (either to act or to be acted upon), so by the mere juxtaposition of the soul, Nature (Prakṛiti) is changed into the principle called the Great One (Buddhi, intellect)." We are not told how this proximity was caused, by which soul acted upon Nature, and Nature brought soul into bondage by connecting it with matter.

[2] In the system of Valentinus the Gnostic, all men and all substances are divided into three classes: (1.) the spiritual, (2.) the vital, and (3.) the material (*Hylic*). This corresponds to the guṇas of Kapila, and is probably an importation from India.

[3] Cf. Aristotle: "Τῆς μὲν οὐσίας ὑπομενούσης τοῖς δὲ πάθεσι μεταβαλλούσης τοῦτο στοχεῖον καὶ ταύτην τῶν ὄντων τὴν ἀρχὴν φασιν εἶναι" (Metaph., i. 3; Wilson, p. 53).

These *guṇas* are called by Kapila: (1.) *sattwa*, truth or goodness; (2.) *rajas*, properly passion, but sometimes interpreted as foulness; and (3.) *tamas*, darkness. Professor Lassen translates them as (1.) essentia, (2.) impetus, (3.) caligo. The first, however, is not more an essence than the second or third. The second, "passion," is rather the cause of an impetus than the impetus itself, the moving force rather than the motion. The terms have, however, only a relative meaning. The *guṇas* [1] are the constituents of Nature, which is only matter, and this is incapable of truth or goodness, according to our ideas of them. *Sattwa* means primarily existence or reality, the real essence of anything, and hence truth and also goodness or virtue; but as by the essence of a being we imply something more subtle than the gross form, the word is used to denote that constituent or formative element of Nature which is lighter and more subtle than the other two. The second constituent is termed "passion" or "foulness," because it is the exciting element, and all action is, to the Hindū mind, an evil, or at least a defect. The perfect state is an inactive repose. The third, "darkness," is the grossest of the elements.

The *guṇas* or modes are sometimes termed (1.) *Prakāśa*,

[1] In the notes to the Sānkhya Kārikā which Lassen has given he explains the word *guṇa* thus: "Diversus sane est usus vocabuli, quum, veluti per Manum, de peculiari cujusvis elementi virtute dicatur. Atque est sane *guṇa* apud Sankyicos materiæ innata ἐνέργεια, per tres gradus ascendens atque considens. Sunt tres materiæ cum arcu vel lyra comparatæ tensiones, et reddi possit *guṇa* haud inepte per potentiam" (p. 30). This is not strictly correct. *Guṇa* means primarily a thread or cord, and Prakṛiti, or Nature, is as a string composed of three varying strands; not properly energies, but constituent elements of different virtue. Kapila did not resolve matter into mere force, as some of our modern physicists. Force was only to him a condition of matter, or rather of one of its primary elements, *i.e.*, of the *guṇa* called "passion."

luminousness; this is prevalent in fire. (2.) *Pravṛitti*, activity; this predominates in air. (3.) *Moha*, delusion; this resides in earth, which, being heavy, is supposed to be formed by, and to represent, the gross, stupefying element.

Every kind of existence except soul is formed by the *guṇas*, but in an infinite variety of conditions, as the different kinds of these elements are blended together in varying degrees.[1]

Kapila, or his disciple, Īśwara Kṛishṇa, proceeds to define more fully the qualities which belong to every one of the twenty-three principles or forms of material existence.

Each is *indiscriminative*, *i.e.*, it has not the power of discerning the differences of things and deciding upon them. The *manas* ("mind") receives the sensations which are caused by the action of external things on the organs of sense; these it transmits to the consciousness (*ahaṅkara*), which presents them to the intellect (*buddhi*). There the soul beholds them as in a mirror. The soul alone discriminates and uses them. Thus only is a true cognition formed.

It is *objective*. The only proper subject is the soul. All other things, from intellect to the grossest form of matter, lie without the soul and are its objects.

It is *generic* (*sāmānya*), *i.e.*, it produces generic or

[1] Even the gods are represented in the Vāyu Purāṇa as springing from the three *guṇas*. "From Pradhāna (Nature), when agitated, the quality of passion (*rajas*) arose, which was there a stimulating cause, as water is to seeds. When an inequality in the *guṇas* arises, then they (the gods) who preside over them are generated. . . . The *rajas* quality was born as Brahmā; the *tamas* (darkness) as Agni; the *sattwa* (goodness) as Vishṇu" (Muir, Sans. Texts, i. 75).

specific forms. Colebrooke translates the word "common," and Gauḍapāda says that it is so called "from being the common possession of all, as a harlot." This is not true, as an exposition of Kapila's system, for *buddhi* is not common to all things. The meaning is, that each may form, with others, things that have common properties.

It is *irrational* (*achetana*, unthinking). Even "intellect" cannot think, for it is material. It is only a passive receptacle for arranged and individualised ideas. Cognition is a property of the soul alone.

It is *productive.* Intellect produces Consciousness, and this produces the five subtle elements, from which the grosser elements proceed.

Nature (*Prakṛiti*) is the same in these respects as each of its developments. Soul, however, is the opposite of Nature. It discriminates; it exists by and for itself alone; it knows, and is not productive.

In Distich 12 the guṇas are classed as pleasant, unpleasant, and stupefying. "Goodness" serves for manifestation, for it is light and elastic; "passion" leads to activity, and "darkness" to restraint or inertness.

Each may subdue or support the other; they are capable of producing each other, and have a mutual existence, *i.e.*, they pass into one another, or produce the effects of each in different conditions; as a good king rewards a good and punishes a bad subject, and clouds which may be heavy and inert may cause fertility and gladness. In their mutual co-operation they are compared to a lamp, whose light is produced by the application of flame to the wick and the oil.

14. "The absence of discrimination and the rest

(the other conditions of material forms) are a conclusion from the three modes, and by the absence of the reverse of this (the modal existence). The Unmanifested (Nature) is also to be determined by the cause having the same qualities as the effect."

In Distich 8 it is affirmed that the productions (emanations) of Nature are in some respects like, and in others unlike, their original source. In Distich 10 the points of disagreement are mentioned, and the points of agreement in Distich 11. The first-named of the common properties is the presence of the three modes, and in Distichs 12 and 13 the nature of these modes is defined. As they affect the constitution of all Nature's productions, the faculty of discrimination cannot belong to any, for this does not belong to the modes. In like manner they are all, from intellect downward, objective, and have other properties of the modes. Also, as they are objective, *i.e.*, external to soul, they must be material.

The latter part of the first line of the distich—tad-viparyayābhāvāt—is obscure. Colebrooke translates it, "and by the absence thereof in the reverse;" that is, as Vāchaspati and others interpret it, in the soul; soul and matter being opposite in their nature. Gauḍapāda confines the passage to the undeveloped Nature (*avyakta*) and the developed principles (*vyakta*), and explains it to mean that the absence of the reverse of these qualities in the developed establishes its absence in the undeveloped, for they are not contrary to each other. Vāchaspati says, also, that "it may be understood as taking for its own two subjects, *vyakta* and *avyakta*, and asserting by the inverted proposition (negatively) that there is no reason (to the contrary) from one being exempt from the three modes."[1] Lassen connects "this" with "the three modes," and after examining other translations, interprets the passage thus: "Quæritur, quomodo interpreter hæc verba; vertenda sunt Latine, quia non est contrarium hujus (*i.e.*, trium qualitatum). Refero autem ad Evolutum et Involutum, de quibus hic potissimum est sermo. Sensus ijitur ex mea opinione est: quia in eis (Involuto et Evoluto) non sunt proprietates tribus qualitatibus contrapositæ. Hæ enim si essent, falsa esset enunciatio dist. 11 proposita." I adopt Lassen's explanation, as best suited to the grammar of the language and to the sequence of ideas, the 14th distich being thus linked to the preceding.

After arguing that the undeveloped (Prakṛiti or Nature), assuming it to exist, must be essentially the same as the developed (forms), five arguments are offered to prove the existence of Prakṛiti.

15. "From the finite nature of specific objects; from the homogeneous nature (of genera and species); from the active energy of evolution (the constant progressive development of finite forms);[2] from the separateness of cause and effect; and from the undividedness (or real unity) of the whole universe."[3]

[1] Wilson, p. 59.

[2] "Propter manifestationem per potestatem" (Lassen); "since effects exist through energy" (Colebrooke); "de l'activité de tout ce qui a puissance d'agir" (St. Hiliare.), lit. from the energetic action (*śakti*) of production or development (*pravṛitti*).

[3] "Since there is a reunion of the universe" (Coleb.); "propter inseparabilitatem omnes formas induentis (Involuti)" (Lassen). *Vaiswarūpa* is the entirety of formal existence.

16. "(It is proved that) there is a primary cause, the Unmanifested (*Avyakta*), which acts (or develops itself) by the three modes; by blending and modification, like water, from the difference of the receptacle or seat of the modes as they are variously distributed."[1]

1. From the finite nature (*parimāṇa*, measure) of specific objects. On this account they must have a cause, for otherwise they would have no limit in space or time. That which is conditioned must be dependent on something external to itself, and be limited by it.

2. From the common properties (*samanvaya*) in different things. Hence species and genera exist, from which we rise to the conception of one primary genus.

3. From the active or living energy (*śakti*) shown in production (emanation) of things. All things are in a state of progression, but their active, progressive life is not due, according to Kapila, to any "potentiality" which they possess in their separate nature.[2] Development implies a developing principle or energy, and this must be from an external source. The arrangement of parts can no more create a living energy than a machine can supply its own motive power.

4. From the separate existence of cause and effect.

[1] "Per diversitatem cujusvis, quam amplectitur qualitatis" (Lassen). "For different objects are diversified by the influence of the several qualities respectively" (Coleb.). Wilson's suggested correction, "by modification, like water, according to the receptacle or subject of the qualities," is certainly correct. This is Gauḍapāda's explanation.

[2] As Lassen explains it: "Evolvuntur evoluta non per suam ipsorum facultatem, sed per potentiam quandam, quæ est causa potestate ea evolvendi instructa" (p. 33).

This is closely connected with the former argument. A living energy is at work in production. This is the producing cause, and we can only conceive of cause and effect as different things, though each is enfolded in the other. The existing world of finite forms is an effect, and must therefore have a cause beyond itself.

5. From the inseparable unity of all (material) forms (*vaisvarūpa*), or of the whole universe in its manifold forms. No part of Nature can exist independently of the rest. There is an unbroken chain or absolute continuity from the lowest to the highest. At the end of the existing *kalpa* (period of creation) they will all become one again. Gauḍapāda assumes this fact as a proof or illustration of the argument. Kapila, however, more logically, refers only to the actual connection of all the several parts of Nature as a proof that they have sprung from a common origin.

Some important questions are suggested by this theory of a primordial matter, from which all things, except soul, have emanated. How does this universal Nature, being one, produce different effects? How does it act at all, since it is not acted upon by anything external to itself? The answer of Kapila is, that it acts by virtue of its internal formation. It is composed of the three *guṇas* or modes, and is inert when these are in equilibrium. It acts through a disturbance of this state. The modes are endowed with a power of motion,[1] like the atoms of Lucretius, and from their restless action combination may be effected in different proportions, as

[1] Motion, however, is primarily due to the mode or constituent element of Nature (Prakṛiti), called "passion" or "foulness."

one or another may be predominant. This is the mixture or blending mentioned in Distich 16. It is also modified, as water or moisture, by different conditions, caused by the nature of its receptacle or seat. "As simple water coming from the clouds is modified as sweet, sour, bitter, pungent, in the nature of the juice of the cocoa-nut, palm, bel-karanja,[1] and wood-apple."

"Modified condition," says Vāchaspati, "is the character of the three modes, which are never for a moment stationary." This constant motion produces different effects by the ever-varying proportion of their action. In the gods, the quality of "goodness" predominates, and they are happy; in mankind, that of "passion" or "foulness," and they are miserable; in animals and lower substances, "darkness" prevails, and they are insensible or indifferent.

Kapila having endeavoured to prove the existence of Nature (*Prakṛiti*), now attempts to prove the existence of soul.

17. "Because an assemblage (of things) is for the sake of another;[2] because the opposite of the three modes and the rest (their modifications) must exist; because there must be a superintending power; because there must be a nature that enjoys; and because of (the existence of) active

[1] The *bel-karanja* is a leguminous plant, whose seed produces an oil used for the cure of scabies (Asiat. Res., iv. 310). A Sanskrit name of the plant is *chiravilwa*.

[2] This is stated a little more fully in the Sānkhya Pravachana: "Every assemblage, every combination, has always for its object another being" (i. 133).

exertion for the sake of abstraction or isolation (from material contact);[1] therefore soul exists."

1. The first argument is from design; not of a designing *mind* from evidences of design, but objectively of another nature for which the arrangement (*saṁghāta*, collocation) of material things is made. "In like manner," says Gauḍapāda, "as a bed, which is an assemblage of bedding, props, cotton, coverlet, and pillows, is for another's use, not for its own, and its several component parts render no mutual service; thence it is concluded that there is a man who sleeps upon the bed, and for whose sake it was made: so this world, which is an assemblage of the five elements, is for another's use; or there is a soul, for whose enjoyment this enjoyable body, consisting of intellect and the rest, has been produced."[2]

2. Because there must be something different from *Prakṛiti* (Nature) formed of the three modes; for this is the material source of pleasure or pain, and the sentient nature, which feels the pleasure or the pain, must be diverse from it.[3] This argument is based upon

[1] Colebrooke translates the last clause, "since there is a tendency to abstraction;" St. Hilaire by "parcequ'enfin il y a une activité qui tend à la liberation absolue des trois espèces de douleurs;" Lassen has "ex actione propter abstractionis causam."

[2] Wilson, p. 66.

[3] Wilson, p. 67. The soul, however, in the Sānkhya system, is not properly sentient, and the difficulty is thus explained in the S. Pravachana (vi. 11): "Though it (pain) is the property or function of something else, yet it is effected (in the soul) by non-distinction (of soul and matter)," or, as the passage is explained by Vijnāna Bhikshu, "though the qualities pleasure, pain, &c., belong only to the *mind* [which is material], they exist in the shape of a *reflection* in it (the soul), through 'non-distinction' as the cause."

our consciousness. We are conscious of a nature within us, which feels joy or woe; and this we infer is something different from matter, for we cannot conceive of mere matter as feeling or thinking.

3. There must be a superintending or directing force. "As a charioteer guides a chariot drawn by horses," says Gauḍapāda, "so the soul guides the body." The idea of Kapila seems to be that the power of self-control cannot be predicated of matter, which must be directed and controlled for the accomplishment of any purpose, and this controlling power must be something external to matter and diverse from it. The soul, however, never acts. It only seems to act; and it is difficult to reconcile this part of the system with that which gives to the soul a controlling force. If the soul is a charioteer, it must be an active agent.

4. "Because there must be a nature that enjoys." This is substantially the same as the first proposition.[1] Gauḍapāda has practically joined them together by a common interpretation. The difference seems to be merely this: That the first refers to an arrangement of utility, and implies that it has been made for some one's use. The fourth indicates ownership or possession, and therefore a possessor, as an estate implies an owner. The idea that underlies both is expressed in the S. Tattwa Kaumudī: "Intellect and the rest are things to

[1] The first or teleological argument appears to be of an universal kind. Every arrangement of material things is for a purpose, and therefore for one in whom that purpose is fulfilled; or, in other words, the use implies an user. Some things, however, as intellect, are evidently, in their nature, an appanage; they have no *raison d'être* except as the adjuncts of another nature, whose ministers they are. They are intermediaries, implying the existence of the two extremes, the objective world and soul.

be enjoyed (*bhogya*, what is eaten, enjoyed, possessed) or perceived (*driśya*), and therefore these imply one that perceives."[1] Each has a separate function, which can only be brought into action by the influence of soul.

5. It is assumed here that the yearning which all sometimes feel for a higher life than we can have in our present bodily state points to the possibility of gaining it. This pure isolation or abstraction (*kaivalya*) from matter cannot be obtained by any material means. These can only work by some kind of material contact, and this is the very condition that makes such a life impossible. The agent, therefore, which must set us free from matter must be something that is not of a material nature. It is knowledge, which the soul gains by its own powers, when brought into proximity to matter.

Kapila, or his expositor Īśwara Kṛishṇa, proceeds to establish the plurality or separate existence of souls.

18. "From the separate allotment of birth, death, and the organs; from the diversity of occupations at the same time, and also from the different conditions (or modifications) of the three modes, it is proved that there is a plurality of souls."[2]

[1] S. Tattwa Kaumudī, Wilson, p. 67.

[2] Neither Hindū nor European commentators explain clearly the meaning of this distich; they merely repeat it. There is, however, the difficulty that the soul is not affected by the three modes. How, then, can their various modifications prove the individuality of souls, in opposition to the Vedāntist doctrine that all souls are only portions of the one, an infinitely extended monad? Kapila's argument seems to be that every soul is accompanied by its liṅga, a subtle body formed of the finer principles of matter, in which lie the dispositions (*bhāvās*) of the individual. Now the liṅga is variously affected by the three modes,

As birth is only the entrance of the soul into another body, and death the departure of the soul from it, then, it is argued, if soul were absolutely one (as the Vedāntists teach), it would enter into bodies or leave them at the same time. It is not very clear why the organs of sense or of action must be alike in all if soul were absolutely one. The course of thought in the mind of Kapila was possibly this: As defects in the organs, such as blindness or deafness, are due to the actions of a previous life, and oneness of soul must produce an uniformity of conditions, such an effect happening to one must happen to all. But all actions are not alike, nor are they the same at the same time, as they would be if all souls (and there is a directing force in the soul) were absolutely one. Men are differently affected, too, by the modes or constituent elements of Nature: one has more affinity to, or is more easily affected by, the mode called "goodness;" another by the mode called "passion;" and another by the "darkness" mode. But if all souls were absolutely one, each person would be the same in his mental and moral state. Each soul has, therefore, a distinct personality, for men are not the same in these respects. This line of argument makes the soul less passive than it is represented to be in other parts of the system, for a certain responsibility is given to it which is inconsistent with the idea of a perfect abstinence from all action.

In the Sānkhya Sūtras (i. 154), Kapila is represented as arguing that his doctrine is not different from that of the Vedas, because the latter are said to teach

and hence arise the different mental and moral conditions of persons, and by this difference each soul is separated from other souls. This, however, is very like saying that men are differentiated from each other, not by their self-consciousness, but by the clothes which they wear

only a *generic* oneness of soul. The sūtra is probably a late interpolation, due to some one who wished to reconcile the system of Kapila with that of the Vedāntist school.[1] Kapila himself seems to have been too honest and too bold a thinker to make such an attempt. The teaching of the Vedānta system is that all souls are one, not because they belong to the same genus or class of being, but because they are portions of the One Spirit, who is indeed the All. Kapila thought that each soul is a separate ens or existence,[2] limited by its union with a body, though soul, in the abstract idea of it, seems to be unlimited. But this abstract soul is not the Supreme Spirit, the Īśwara or Lord of the Pantajali system. If an absolute Supreme Spirit exists, he maintained (it seems) that such a nature lies outside the domain of philosophy; humanity being with him, as with Fichte and the Comtists, the highest point of philosophic research.

19. "And from that contrariety (of soul) it is concluded that the witnessing soul is isolated, neutral, perceptive, and inactive by nature."

[1] The Vedāntist leaning of the Sānk. Pravachana shows not only that Kapila was not the author of the work, but that it is later in time than the Sānk. Kārikā.

[2] Cf. Sānk. Pravachana (vi. 63), where it is said that the separate life of a soul (*jīvatwa*, the property of living) is from a distinction as of race, *i.e.*, by attendant qualities; or, as Vijnāna Bhikshu interprets the passage, "to be a living soul means the being possessed of the vital airs (see p. 66), and this is the character of the soul distinguished by personality, not of pure soul (which is unconditioned)." There is some confusion here. In the system of Kapila the vital airs belong to the body and do not affect the soul. In the next Sutra all action is separated from the soul and from any superintending influence. "The accomplishment of works depends on the agent, self-consciousness (see p. 18), not on a Lord (Īśwara), from the absence of proof (that such a Lord exists)."

20. "It is thus, from this union, that the unintelligent body (the *liṅga*)[1] appears to be intelligent, and from the activity of the modes the stranger (the soul) appears to be an agent."

21. "It is that the soul may be able to contemplate Nature, and to become entirely separated from it, that the union of both is made, as of the halt and the blind, and through that (union) the universe is formed."

The soul beholds as an eye-witness (*sākshin*), for insight or cognition does not belong to matter. "That which is irrational cannot observe, and that to which an object is apparent is a witness." It is *solitary* or perfectly distinct from matter, and therefore from the modifications which the modes produce. It is *neutral* (*mādhyastha*, lit. standing between), "as a wandering ascetic is lonely and unconcerned while the villagers are busily engaged in agriculture."[2] It is *perceptive*. This appears to differ from the first quality in this, that as a witness the soul only observes, and then by seeing that which is presented to it by the *buddhi* (intellect), it perceives and understands the phenomena of the material world. It is still, however, passive or inert. All action, in the judgment of a Hindū, is inferior to a contemplative state, and the soul in its regal

[1] Prof. Wilson says: "The term *liṅga* in the first line is explained to denote *mahat* [intellect] and the subtle products of *pradhāna* [Nature]." This is a mistake. The *liṅga* does not denote them. This subtle vehicle of the soul is formed from the substance of the three internal organs and the finer elements of matter (*tanmātra*).

[2] Gauḍapāda's Commentary.

grandeur has no part in the inferior life of action. It directs as a sovereign, but it does not work. In the system of Kapila, all action, even mental effort or application, is due to the influence of the three modes, of which Nature (*Prakṛiti*) is formed, and the soul is not subject to their influence. It is, therefore, completely passive.[1]

In every form of earthly life the soul is united to its own peculiar vehicle or body, but is not blended with it; it is only in a state of juxtaposition, or rather it is enveloped by the body. By this is meant, not the gross material body, which perishes at each migration of the soul, but the *liṅga,* which is formed out of the subtler elements of Nature. This attends the soul until finally a complete separation from matter is obtained.

It is from the proximity of "intellect" (*buddhi*) to the soul that the former seems to think and the latter to act. "Thence," says the S. Chandrikā, "that which is an effect of *pradhāna* (Nature), the category, *buddhi,* though it is unintelligent, is as if it were intelligent: says, 'I know,' and is endowed with knowledge." But there is no true cognition until the soul has seen the individualised and complete sensations, now elaborated into form, in the *buddhi.* It is from this effect that the soul seems to act, the motive power of the "intellect" being in close approximation to it. It has, indeed, a kind of action in itself, so far as observation and the formation of thought are action, but it is not an agent upon anything external to itself. Kapila insists upon this distinction, which is

[1] "To fools the spirit seems to be active, when the senses alone are really active; just as the moon appears to move when the clouds only are passing" (Atma Bōdha Prakāsika, by Śankara-āchārya, i. 19, quoted in Ind. Ant., May 1876).

essential to his system, from a strong conviction of the absolute and essential distinction of soul and matter. They are in their very nature subject and object, and can never coalesce. As "idea" and "thing" they are eternally separate, and their properties or functions can never be interchanged. The doctrine of Fichte—that material things exist, at least to us, only as a result of the laws of the inward subjective nature—is wholly contrary to that of Kapila. Both are absolute entities, having distinct functions, but it is only by the juxtaposition of the two that knowledge can be gained. This is a result of the synthesis of the discerning faculty and the thing to be discerned. Hence there are no innate ideas, and the soul, when freed from the contact of matter, has neither knowledge nor self-consciousness. The soul can only see what *buddhi* (intellect) presents to its view, and it is of the essence of his system that "nihil est in intellectu, quod non prius in sensu." In making the soul absolutely dependent on the senses for its ideas; in refusing to admit that there is anything higher than the individual soul which may enlighten or act upon it, he laid the foundation for a philosophical atheism, or what is now called agnosticism. Like Fichte, in making the individual self, *i.e.*, the soul, the highest form of knowable being, he rejected the idea of a supreme, personal Deity, as a truth determined by logical inference, though it is not certain that he absolutely denied it. We cannot know God, because he cannot be presented as an object to be seen in the *buddhi*, and the soul has no virtue or moral consciousness, for this is a property of our material nature. He seems to magnify philosophy, as an outcome of human reason, as some of our modern teachers, but in reality degrades it, both in its mental and moral aspects, by making the thinking faculty completely dependent on the sensations that come from material things for the whole of its knowledge, and even its self-consciousness.

Kapila teaches (Dist. 21) that the material universe was formed, or, in Hindū phrase, the various forms of matter were evolved, by the unconscious *Prakṛiti* (Nature), for the use of the soul, *i.e.*, that the soul may gain a knowledge of material things, and thus by contrast know itself as the means of a final liberation from matter. This is illustrated by the well-known tale of a blind man meeting in a forest with one that was lame, when, agreeing to help each other, the blind man bore the lame on his shoulders, and by the union of their powers they were able to escape from the jungle. Nature (*Prakṛiti*) is the blind man, for it cannot see, and the soul is the lame one, for it cannot act.

The order in which the various emanations from Nature were produced is then set forth—

22. "From Nature (*Prakṛiti*) issues the great principle (*mahat*, intellect), and from this the Ego or Consciousness; from this (consciousness) the whole assemblage of the sixteen (principles or entities), and from five of the sixteen the five gross elements."

The categories, or separate entities, of the Sānkhya system have been assumed in the previous distichs, and their mutual relations determined. Here the order of their production is given. This has been stated in p. 17 ff., but it may be useful to present it in a tabular form.

1. Prakṛiti or primordial matter, the ὕλη of the Greek philosophy.

2. Mahat or Buddhi (intellect).

3. Ahankāra, the Ego or Consciousness.

4. The five subtle elements (Tanmātra).

5. The five grosser elements, ether, air, earth, light or fire, and water.

6. The five senses.

7. The five organs of action.

8. The Manas (mind), which is the first of the internal organs, receiving the impressions made upon the senses. It ought to be numbered with *buddhi* and *ahaṅkāra*, making with them the three internal organs.

9. The soul (*Ātman, Purusha*), which is totally distinct from Prakṛiti (Nature), forms, with Nature and its emanations, the twenty-five *tattwas* (categories) in the Sānkhya philosophy. He who understands them thoroughly has attained to the highest state of man in the present life, and in laying aside the body in death shall know birth no more: he is for ever freed from any contact with matter, and therefore from pain. "He who knows the twenty-five principles, whatever order of life he may enter, and whether he wear braided hair, or a top-knot only, or be shaven, he is free; of this there is no doubt."[1]

23. "Intellect is the distinguishing principle (*adhyavasāya*). Virtue, knowledge, freedom from passion, and power denote it when affected by (the

[1] Quoted in Gauḍapāda's Comm. (Wilson, p. 79). The meaning is, whether he has the braided or matted hair worn by Śiva and ascetics, or be a Brāhman, or has the shaven head (muṇḍa) of a Buddhist.

mode) 'goodness;' when affected by 'darkness' it is the reverse of these."

The word by which *buddhi* (intellect) is defined or explained is unfortunately of doubtful meaning. In the Amara Kosha it is a synonym of *utsāha,* strenuous effort.[1] The Peters. Dict. interprets it by "fester wille," "fester bestreben." Professor Lassen translates it by "intentio," and Colebrooke by "ascertainment." St. Hilaire writes, "L'intelligence, c'est la determination distincte des choses," and with this interpretation the comment of Gauḍapāda agrees.[2] "This is a jar, this is cloth; that which marks or designates thus is *buddhi.*" The word is, however, more commonly used in the sense of "determination," "resolve;" but this appears to be a secondary meaning, the primary being a defining or distinguishing act. "Intellect" (*buddhi*) is then, in the system of Kapila, the faculty or organ by which outward objects are presented to the view of the soul in their proper and definite form. Some of the commentators suppose that here is the seat of will, or that by *buddhi* we say, "This must be done." But this assignment is probably due to the modern sense of the word; for it does not appear that Kapila attributed volition to any form of matter, though as subtle as that of *buddhi.*

He assigns to it, however, other properties which are equally strange as attributes of matter. Having defined the soul as that which contemplates but never acts, he is

[1] It has this meaning in the Hitopadeśa, "effort," "determined application" (see Voc. by Johnson).

[2] The same word is used to denote *buddhi* in the S. Parv. Bhāshna, and is interpreted by Dr. Ballantyne as "judgment." "Intellect is judgment, and judgment, called also ascertainment, is its peculiar modification" (ii. 13).

obliged to assign every quality or state that is connected with our active life to *buddhi*, the first emanation of Prakṛiti (Nature), as its primary seat. When it is under the influence of that mode or constituent of Nature called "goodness," it is (1.) virtue (*dharma*), (2.) knowledge (*jnāna*), (3.) absence of passion or passivity (*virāga*), and (4.) supernatural power (*aiśwarya*). When affected by the mode called "darkness," it is then vice, ignorance, passion, and weakness. The commentators, who are generally under a Vedāntist influence, explain virtue (*dharma*) as including humanity, benevolence, acts of restraint (*yama*) and of obligation (*niyama*). Gauḍapāda explains acts of restraint as restraint of cruelty, falsehood, dishonesty, incontinence, and avarice; acts of obligation are purification, contentment, religious austerities, sacred study and divine worship; but he expressly refers this interpretation to the Pātanjala, or theistic branch of the Sānkhya school. Knowledge, according to the same commentator, is of two kinds, external and internal. The former includes knowledge of the Vedas and the six branches of study connected with them—recitation, ritual, grammar, interpretation of words, prosody, and astronomy; also of the Purāṇas, and of logic, theology, and law. Internal knowledge is the knowledge of Nature (*Prakṛiti*) and soul, or the discrimination that "This is Nature," the equipoised condition of the modes; and "This is Soul," devoid of modes, pervading,[1] and intelligent. By external knowledge worldly distinction or admiration is obtained;

[1] Gauḍapāda gives this attribute to the soul, the power of pervading (vyāpī); but this is properly a Vedāntist idea. Kapila attributes much supernatural power to the soul in certain states, but he does not assign the power of pervading matter as its constant attribute.

by internal knowledge, liberation, *i.e.*, from the bondage of matter.

Kapila, however, placed a knowledge of the Vedas at a very low point, if he did not discard it altogether. Religious austerities and divine worship found no place in his system. The soul of man is the highest existence which his philosophy contemplates, recognising, as Comtism, only the supremacy of humanity, but rising above M. Comte in admitting the soul to be its only true representative.

Dispassion is also of two kinds—one which is indifference to all external things, either on account of their defects, or the trouble of acquiring them, or their injuriousness and wrong; and another which seeks only to be delivered from matter, accounted as "illusion,"[1] that the soul may be free.

By "power" or "mastery" is meant (we are told) supernatural or magical power. A devotee who shall attain, by knowledge, to a complete abstraction from anything external to himself, can accomplish what he pleases: he may traverse all things by subtlety of Nature; may rise to colossal dimensions; may stand on the tops of the filaments of a flower; may rise to the solar sphere on a sunbeam, and may command the three worlds. Whatever the person having this faculty intends or proposes must be complied with by that which is the subject of his purpose; the elements themselves must conform to his designs. "The ordinary laws that govern material

[1] This is Gauḍapāda's interpretation. "Illusion" (*indrajāla*, Indra's net) means a kind of magic, probably at first a kind of mirage arising from the rays of the sun (Indra). Here, as elsewhere, there is a Vedāntist colouring. Wilson renders it "witchcraft."

things," says Hemachandra, "cannot impede the movements of one who has attained to this etherealised state."

24. "Egoism is self-consciousness. From this proceeds a double creation (*sarga*, emanation), the series of the eleven (principles) and the five (subtle) elements."

25. "From consciousness modified (by 'goodness') proceed the eleven good principles;[1] from this origin[2] of being as 'darkness' come the subtle elements. Both emanations are caused by the 'foul' or 'active' mode."[3]

The term used in Distich 24 as the definition of the ego (*ahaṅkāra*) is *abhimāna*. The ordinary meaning of this word is "pride."[4] As Vāchaspati interprets it, "The pride or conceit of individuality, self-sufficiency, the notion that 'I do, I feel, I think, I am, I alone preside, and have

[1] In the Comm. on the S. Pravachana by Vijnāna Bhikshu, *ēkadaśaka* is explained as "eleventh," *i.e.*, the eleventh organ, *manas*, which proceeds from consciousness when modified by goodness.

[2] *Bhūtādi*, rightly translated by Lassen "elementorum generator," the elements being what we call "matter" in its subtler forms. St. Hilaire has, incorrectly, "élément primitif."

[3] *Taijasa*, having the nature of the *tejas*, or active mode.

[4] The ordinary sense of both words (*ahaṅkāra* and *abhimāna*) is pride. The principle is therefore something more in Hindū metaphysics than mere consciousness. "It might be better expressed perhaps by *le moi*, as it adds to the simple conception of individuality the notion of self-property, the concentration of all objects and interests and feelings in the individual" (Wilson, p. 91). The meaning of pride is a secondary one. It is not contained in the philosophical use of the word, which expresses only the perception, not the exaltation, of self; though very naturally this perception led to a sense of superiority over outward things. Lassen gives an explanation of *abhimāna* from a native scholiast: "Abhimāna est persuasio hominis in omnibus rebus semetipsum respici, omniaque ad se spectare" (p. 36).

power over all that is perceived or known, and all these objects of sense for my use: there is no other Supreme, except this ego, I am.' This pride, from its exclusive application, is egotism." We cannot suppose that Kapila meant to imply all this by the term *abhimāna*, but probably he did mean by it that egoism is not merely a consciousness of our individual life, but that which forms the relation we bear to the outer world.

The eleven principles are the organs or faculties of sense and action, together with the *manas* (see p. 21). For the five subtle elements see p. 19.

The physical substratum of consciousness is affected by the modes, as every other emanation of Prakṛiti. From the influence of "goodness," it produces the ten organs and the *manas* which are called "good" because of their utility; but it is only when affected by that mode or constituent of Nature called "darkness"[1] that it produces inanimate matter. The element called "passion," which is here described as ardent or glowing (*taijasa*), must co-operate in the production of all, because it is the exciting mode.

The Egoism of Kapila has a threefold name, according to the various actions of the modes. When the mode called "goodness" affects it, and it produces the eleven good principles—the ten organs and the *manas*—it is

[1] A real darkness is assumed in a splendid hymn of the Rig-Veda (x. 129)—

> "Nor aught nor naught existed; yon bright sky
> Was not, nor heaven's broad woof outstretched above.
> The only One breathed breathless in itself;
> Other than it there nothing since has been.
> Darkness there was, and all at first was veiled
> In gloom profound, an ocean without light."
>
> —*M. Müller's Translation.*

In the old Greek cosmogonies, Erebus or Night was the primordial state from which all things arose.

then called modified (*vaikṛita*) Consciousness. When it is under the influence of the mode "darkness" and produces inanimate matter, it is then called *bhūtādi*, source of elemental being. The influence of the mode called "passion" excites the others to action, for the giving of activity or impetus is its especial office. The three modes therefore act upon, or rather within, egoism or consciousness (for this, as a part of Prakṛiti, or an emanation of it, is itself formed of the modes), and their various action has the effect of producing different results; the first and second modes in union causing the first issue, and the second and third in their joint action the inferior class of existences.

26. "The eye, the ear, the nose, the tongue, and the skin[1] are termed the organs of intellect (*buddhi*); the voice, the hands, the feet, (the organs of) excretion and generation are called the organs of action."

27. "The *manas* (mind) in this respect has the nature of both (classes). It is formative (or determinative), and a sense-organ from having cognate functions (with the other organs). It is multifarious from the specific modifications of the modes and the diversity of external things."[2]

28. "The function of the five (senses), with

[1] Gauḍapāda, whom Wilson follows, has *sparśanaka*, that which touches or has contact; the skin, as a sensitive organ. The MSS., however, have *twach*, the skin, and this is Lassen's reading.

[2] Colebrooke adopts the reading *bāhyabhedaścha* and translates the passage: "They (the organs) are numerous by specific modification of qualities, and so are external diversities." Following the explana-

regard to sound and other (sense-objects), is that of observation only. Speech, handling, walking, excretion, and generation are the functions of the five (organs)."

The eye, the ear, &c., are organs of the intellect (*buddhi*), because they receive sensations which are transmitted through the *manas* to the intellect. In this division the tongue is considered only as the seat of the sensation of taste. The other organs are those of action. The organisation by which speech is produced is classed under this head, and the power or faculty of speech is evidently referred to mere sensation, as handling and walking. Probably Kapila meant to imply that language, at least in its primary form, only expresses what Locke calls "sensible" ideas; *i.e.*, ideas of material things formed by the senses. The action of mind upon language he does not allude to, and as the soul, in the system of Kapila, can only contemplate, it does not appear how language has passed from the expression of material objects to an abstract or spiritual meaning.

The *manas* belongs to both classes. It is both an organ of the intellect and an instrument of action. The word by which its proper function is defined (*saṅkalpaka*) is explained in an uncertain manner by the

tion of Vāchaspati and Gauḍapāda, Lassen has *bahyabhedāchcha* (bhedāt) and translates the line thus: "Multifidum est (the *manas*) propter diversam per qualitates mutationem et propter divisionem per res externas." The MSS. are equally divided as to the reading. As the distich is devoted to an explanation of the *manas*, I prefer, of the two, Lassen's interpretation and the reading on which it is founded, but have given a slightly different version.

Hindū commentators. It is compounded of *sam* (Lat. = *cum*) and *kalpa,* "form," from *kḷip,* to dispose, to prepare. It may be translated as "formative" or "plastic;" the faculty of the *manas* being to collect together and arrange in an idealised form the manifold impressions of the senses.[1] It is the *sensorium commune* in the system of Kapila. The Latin *mens* and our *mind* correspond to it in origin but not in meaning. In our Western philosophy, mind is usually considered as an expression for the rational faculties of the soul, and as opposed to matter; but in the view of Kapila, it is not a part of the soul, but is itself a form of matter from a material source (*Prakṛiti*). Its functions are thus explained by Vāchaspati: "It gives form in a collective manner to that which is perceived by an organ of sense, and says 'This is a thing;' 'This is compounded and that is not so,' and it discriminates or defines (a thing) by its specific or unspecific nature." The *manas* then is the first agent between the outer world and the soul, collecting and shaping the scattered, indefinite sensations of the different organs of sense.

[1] Colebrooke renders the passage thus: "It (the *manas*) ponders, and it is an organ as being cognate with the rest;" but the *manas* never ponders; it is an unconscious agent, whose office is merely to transmit our sense-impressions, when collected and united, through consciousness to the intellect (*buddhi*). It is an organ, not from being cognate merely with the other organs in its origin, but from having cognate duties or functions (*sadharma*) to fulfil. Lassen translates thus: "Geminæ indolis inter hosce sensus est animus (*manas*), et imaginans est." St. Hilaire: "Le cœur (*manas*) est à la fois . . . et un organe d'action et an organ d'intelligence: sa fonction est de reunir." The Hindū commentators seem to have been perplexed by the secondary meaning of *saṅkalpa,* "design," in its twofold sense of a "formed plan" or "project" and "resolve." Hence, too, they have assigned the faculty of will to the *manas,* which in Kapila's system is unconscious and subordinate.

It belongs, however, to that mode or constituent element of Nature (*Prakṛiti*) which is called "goodness." It is, therefore, not dull, inanimate matter, for this proceeds from the mode called "darkness," but matter of a subtle, elastic, animate nature.

The multifariousness mentioned in Distich 27, is often understood to refer to the diversified natures of the ten *organs.* It is so applied by Colebrooke and Professor Wilson after Gauḍapāda. But the distich is evidently devoted to a description of the *manas*, and the multiform action is assigned in the Sānkhya Pravachana Bhāshya more correctly to this organ alone, on which it is imposed by the varying actions of the modes and the variety of external things: "as the same individual assumes different characters according to the influence of his associations, becoming a lover with his beloved, a sage with sages, and a different person with others; so mind (*manas*) becomes various from its connection with the eye or any other organ, being identified with it, and being diversified by the modification of the function of sight and the rest of the organs." If, then, the manas is not in action, the sensation received from an object is lost, or, in the language of Locke, "perception is only when the mind receives the impression." It is thus that the *manas* is both an organ of perception and action; for it receives an impression from the senses and then actively forms this impression, which before "was only as the knowledge of a child or a dumb man," into a definite form according to its properties or its species.

The function of the five organs of the intellect is that of observation only (*ālochana*, seeing, observing). This cannot be applied literally to all the senses. The meaning appears to be that each organ acts passively in receiving only the sensations which affect it, as the eye receives impressions of form and colour. In the Sānkhya Pravachana it is said that the senses are the instruments of the soul. It is through the action of the *manas* and *buddhi* that the impressions made on the senses become real perceptions, if such a term can be applied to the action of unconscious matter.

29. "The function (or action) of the three (internal organs) is the distinguishing mark (specific nature [1]) of each, and it is not common (to the three). The common (combined) function of these organs is (the production of) the five vital airs, breathing and the rest."

30. "The function (or action) of the four (the internal organs and an organ of sense) is declared to be either instantaneous or consecutive with regard to visible objects; the function of the three (internal organs) with regard to an invisible object is preceded by that of the fourth." [2]

In Distich 29 the distinct individuality of the three internal organs is affirmed, *i.e.*, their functions in the formation of ideas are never interchanged; but they have a common physiological function assigned to them,

[1] *Swālakshaṇyam*, "specifische unterschiedenheit" (Petersburg Dict.).

[2] *Tatpūrvikā vrittih*, not, as Professor Wilson translates it, "their prior function," but the function of the three (internal organs) is preceded by that (the action of a sense-organ).

and that is the maintenance of the five vital "airs."[1] The word employed here (*vāyu*, air or wind) does not mean the elemental air, but a subtle inward force or action, necessary to vitality and independent of sensation. According to Gauḍapāda they are—

1. *Prāna*, breath, the ordinary inspiration and expiration.

2. *Apāna*, downward breath, the air or vital force acting in the lower parts of the body.

3. *Samāna*, collective breath; "so named from conducting equally the food, &c., through the body."

4. *Udāna*, ascending breath, the vital force that causes the pulsations of the arteries in the upper portions of the body from the navel to the head.

5. *Vyāna*, separate breath, "by which internal division and diffusion through the body are effected."[2] This is not very intelligible, but as *vyāna* is connected in the S. Tattwa Kaumudī with the skin, the subtle nerve-force by which sensibility is given to the skin or outer surface of the body is probably meant. It is also connected with the circulation of the blood along the surface, the great arteries being under the action of *udāna*.[3]

In the absence of a precise definition of these "airs," a variety of fanciful explanations is furnished by native

[1] The maintenance of the five vital airs is attributed by Gauḍapāda to all the organs, but by the Hindū commentators generally to the three internal organs exclusively. Vijnāna Bhikhsu, in his commentary on the Sānkhya Pravachana, expressly limits the production and continuance of the vital airs to the three internal organs (ii. 31).

[2] Gauḍapāda, Wilson, p. 105.

[3] In the Ātma-bodha (knowledge of the soul), a Vedāntic poem assigned to the great commentator Śankarāchārya, the soul is said to be enwrapped "in five investing sheaths or coverings" (*kośha*, cf. Fr. *cosse*; Ir. Gael. *coch-al*, a pod or husk). The third of these is called *prāṇa-maya*, *i.e.*, "the sheath composed of breath, and the other vital airs associated with the organs of action" (Indian Wisdom, p. 123).

commentators. It is evident that they denote some subtle forces which cause respiration, excretion, digestion, the circulation of the blood, and the sensibility of the skin —an unsatisfactory kind of physiology; but here is the first germ of the science, and the "airs" of Kapila are as scientific as the "vapours" which in the opinion of our forefathers caused melancholy and other diseases. They indicate a dim perception of what we call "nerve-force," something more subtle than the elements of inanimate matter; for it is caused by the action of the internal organs, which are due to the agency of the mode called "goodness," *i.e.*, matter of an etherealised and animate kind.

The action of the internal organs and sensation may be either instantaneous, like a flash of lightning, or gradual; "as," says Gauḍapāda, "a person going along a road sees an object at a distance, and is in doubt whether it be a post or a man; he then observes some characteristic marks upon it, or a bird perched there, and doubt being thus dissipated by the reflection of the mind, the understanding (*buddhi*) discriminates that it is a post;[1] and then egotism interposes for the sake of certainty, as "Verily (or I am certain) it is a post." In this way the functions of intellect, egotism, mind (*manas*), and the eye are (successively) fulfilled. The doctrine of the Vaiśeshikas was that, in all cases, the formation of ideas is a gradual process.

This observation will apply to objects that are within

[1] This is Professor Wilson's translation of the passage. I venture to translate it: "A doubt (or doubtful impression) having been formed by the *manas*, the intellect (*buddhi*) becomes discriminative." The *manas* does not reflect; it only forms a *saṅkalpa*, or collected form of an object from the sensory impressions.

the range of the senses at a given time. If the object be not present, then the reproduction of an idea is dependent on memory, for which a previous sensation is necessary. Memory is therefore a revived sensation; it is assumed that this has been, by some means, unconsciously retained.

Kapila seems to teach herein that "nihil est in intellectu quod non prius in sensu;" but not wholly so. He also would add, "Nisi intellectus ipse." The soul has a distinct faculty, which belongs to its own nature and is independent of the inner or outer organs. It sees and understands the forms of external things presented by its ministers, the internal organs. The soul alone is the seat of all real cognition; it alone knows and decides; it is therefore something more than a name for a generalisation of the nerve-processes of the brain, as some of our modern physiologists affirm "mind" to be.

31. "They (the internal organs) perform each his own separate function, which is caused to act by a mutual impulse. The advantage of the soul is their cause of action. An organ is not caused to act by any one."

The organs are defined and separate in their functions, but act upon each other by a mutual impulse (*ākūta*[1]).

[1] *Ākūta* is glossed in the Petersb. Lexicon by *absicht*, *antrieb*. Colebrooke's translation is "incited by mutual invitation." Lassen has "ad quam cietur unum *ratione* alterius." The meaning of "incitement to activity," mentioned by Wilson, expresses more nearly the sense of *ākūta*. "L'influence spontanée qu'ils exercent les uns sur les autres" (St. Hilaire). It is composed of *ā*, to, towards, and *kū*, to cry. Gauḍapāda says that it means *ādarasambhrama* (respectful eagerness in action).

Colebrooke and Wilson suppose that in this distich all the organs are referred to, but Gauḍapāda, more correctly, I think, connects it with the three internal organs only.

This word generally implies a conscious purpose or resolve; but as the organs are not intelligent, the term is explained to mean an unconscious activity which is produced by the action of one organ upon another for the fulfilment of a design which is common to them all, and this is the final liberation of the soul from matter. For this purpose they act spontaneously but unconsciously, as the milk of a cow is formed unconsciously in the udder and yet serves to nourish the calf. They act, however, by an impulse derived from their own nature, and cannot be directed by any external agent.

32. "Instrument (or organ) is of thirteen kinds, and has the property of seizing, retaining, and manifesting: the effect to be produced is of ten kinds, and is that which is to be seized, retained, or manifested."

33. "The internal organs are three; the external ten,[1] and these are to make known external objects to the three (internal organs). The external organs act only at the time present; the internal (or intermediate) at the three divisions of time."

Gauḍapāda refers the property of manifestation to the organs of the intellect only, and those of seizing and holding to the organs of action. Professor Wilson adopts this view; but the author of the "Kārikā" appears to

[1] St. Hilaire translates this part "l'exterieur [organe] est *simple*," but for what reasons he does not say. The text is *daśadhā vahyam*, "the external (set of organs) is in ten divisions."

attribute these properties to all the organs alike. The organ of sight seizes and holds the impression conveyed by an external object and manifests it to the *manas;* this organ does the same to consciousness, and the latter to the intellect (*buddhi*), which, as a mirror, receives, retains, and reflects the impression, which has now become a definite ideal form, that the soul may see it. The ten external organs are the means of making external objects known to the internal, but they are limited in their action to the present time, the eye receiving an impression only from an object then present; but the internal organs have relation to time past, present, and future. This would seem to imply that they possess within themselves a power of volition, and that they are the seat of memory. The *manas* and the other internal organs appear to have impressions stamped, or (so to speak) photographed upon them; and these may be reproduced without reference to time. But Kapila has not attempted to determine where the power of willing resides, nor has he treated of memory or imagination as a distinct faculty. If the soul really directs, "as a charioteer directs a chariot," then it acts, though not as a mechanical force, and the faculty of volition must belong to it. But the action of the internal organs in reproducing a previous impression is not expressly referred to the soul, but rather to the organs themselves, which, though material, are thus endowed with a kind of volition.[1]

[1] In the Sānkhya Pravachana (ii. 39–41) the *manas* is called the chief of the organs, and the possession of memory is assigned as a reason for the distinction. Memory is therefore a quality or function of the *manas.* Gauḍapāda, however, attributes to each of the three internal organs the power of acting according to its own nature without reference to time, and to *buddhi* (intellect) is attributed the power

The results of the action of the organs are tenfold, according to the nature of the five organs of sensation and the five of action.

34. "Of these, the five intellectual organs (or organs of sensation) are the domain[1] of specific and non-specific objects.[2] Speech is connected with sound. The rest are connected with the five objects of sense."

35. "Since the intellect (*buddhi*), with the other internal organs, allies itself[3] with all objects of sense, these three organs are the gatekeepers and the rest are gates."

36. "These having different characteristic (specific) differences from each other, and being variously affected by the modes, present the whole (of being[4]) in the 'intellect' (*buddhi*) for the sake of the soul, enlightening it, having a likeness to a lamp."

37. "As it is 'intellect' which accomplishes all

of forming an idea not only of a present object, but of one past or future; so also consciousness and the *manas* can act, and memory, or imagination, in its complete form, must be a product of the three.

[1] *Vishaya*, gebiet, wirkungskreis (Peters. Dict.). The meaning is, the five intellectual organs have specific and non-specific objects as their province or domain. "Sensuum perficiendi inter hos quinum provinciæ sunt distincta atque indistincta."(Lassen).

[2] See Note A.

[3] *Avagāhate*, "adverts to (C.); "perlustrat" (L.); "embrasse" (St. H.); lit. "dives down to," and thence, "has business with, apprehends."

[4] "Present to the intellect the soul's whole *purpose*" (Colebrooke and Gauḍapāda). "Universitatem genii causa menti tradunt" (Lassen). St. Hilaire has, after Colebrooke, "presentent a l'intelligence l'objet entier de l'âme." I prefer Lassen's version. The organs bring all things in a definite form before the soul, as a lamp reveals objects, that the soul may know both them and itself.

the fruition of the soul, so also it is that which discriminates the subtle difference between the chief principle (*Pradhāna* = *Prakṛiti*) and the soul."

There is much uncertainty about the meaning of the "specific" and "non-specific" objects mentioned in Distich 34. Gauḍapāda, whose explanation is quoted by Professor Wilson, affirms that specific objects are those which are perceived by men, and those which are non-specific are seen only by the gods. This is nothing more than a guess, which proves that the original meaning of the words had been lost. In the 38th distich those objects which have no specific marks are the subtle elements of matter, and Kapila's meaning appears to be (as M. St. Hilaire has suggested), that the organs of sensation (or of "intellect") have a relation to these as well as to the gross elements. For example, the gross element ether is produced from a subtle element called "sound." The doctrine of Kapila seems to be, that in hearing, the ear has a relation not only to the ether, but to the subtler principle that underlies it; a dim apprehension of the truth that hearing depends not only on some channel of communication between the ear and the source of sound, but on some modification of the material element through which the sound is conducted. This explanation is supported by the S. Tattwa Kaumudī, which identifies specific with corporeal objects, and non-specific with subtle, rudimental objects, the latter being seen only by holy men and gods. This clause Kapila would reject, for he set knowledge and philosophers above virtue and holy men, and is silent about the gods. He appears to have supposed that a high power of physical discernment is possible to those who are sufficiently enlightened by knowledge.

Speech has reference only to sound, *i.e.*, we can only hear it; but the remaining four organs of action may be connected with all the five kinds of sensation; "as in the combination of sound, touch, colour, smell, taste in objects like a water-jar and others, which may be taken hold of by the hand." [1]

All the organs are affected by the modes or constituents of Nature; they are only modifications of these three kinds of matter. They may, therefore, cause pleasure, pain, and insensibility.

The succession of the agencies by which the soul is reached is thus stated by Vāchaspati: "As the headmen of the village collect the taxes from the villagers and pay them to the governor of the district; as the local governor pays the amount to the minister, and the minister receives it for the use of the king; so the *manas* having received ideas from the external organs transfers them to consciousness, and consciousness delivers them to intellect (*buddhi*), the general superintendent, who takes charge of them for the use of the sovereign, soul." [2] The intellect is, therefore, the soul's chief officer, its direct agent, and presents all that it receives, as in a mirror, to the gaze of the soul; not for the purpose, however, of adding to its treasures, but simply to free it by knowledge from contact with matter.[3] It has thus the means of discriminating be-

[1] S. Tattwa Kaumudī, Wilson, p. 115.

[2] Wilson, p. 117.

[3] The mental physiology of Kapila is imperfect. The "intellect" (*buddhi*) merely represents sensational ideas in a complete form to the gaze of the soul, and the soul never acts. It does not appear, therefore, how abstract ideas are

tween matter and itself in order to discern its own higher nature. This knowledge does not lead to virtue or piety. Gauḍapāda says that it is gained only by those who practise religious austerities; but here, as in other places, he misinterprets Kapila, to whom religion was neither a means nor an end. It has an inferior place in his system. Virtue and religion may do something, by causing the attainment of a happier birth, but by knowledge only can the soul attain to its final liberation.

38. "From these five subtle elements, which are non-specific, proceed the five gross elements (*bhūtāni*), which are called 'specific.' They are (in their nature) tranquil, violent, and stupefying."

The five gross elements and the five subtle elements which underlie them have been explained in page 20. The subtle elements are said to be non-specific. This is explained to mean that "they have only one quality or mode, which is not affected by change, and by which no feeling of pleasure, pain, or stupidity can be produced." But it belongs to the nature of any mode or constituent of Nature to produce some effect of this kind. Vijnāna Bhikshu explains the term "non-specific" by saying that "the subtle elements are not affected by the modes; that they have an unchanging nature; but the gross elements change in their nature and effects according to circumstances. Thus the wind is agree-

formed, or by what means a course of reasoning can be carried on. The Vedāntists add a fourth faculty called *chitta*, the thinking or reasoning faculty.

able to a person oppressed by heat, disagreeable to one that is cold, and when tempestuous or loaded with clouds of sand or dust, it is stupefying." As the subtle elements never come into contact with the bodily organs, they cannot cause any sensations, of whatever kind, though the gods, and sometimes even sages, may perceive them and receive pleasure from them.[1] They must also be affected by the modes, for these form every development of Nature, as they are from Nature itself. We may best translate these terms by "diversified" and "non-diversified." The subtle elements have each only one nature and one effect. The gross elements may have various effects, and become changed in kind by commingling in various degrees.

39. "Subtle (bodies), those which are born of father and mother, with the gross forms of existence,[2] are the threefold species (of bodies). Of these, the subtle are permanent; those which are born of father and mother perish."

40. "The subtle (body) *liṅga*, formed primevally, unconfined, permanent, composed of 'intellect' and the rest, down to the subtle elements, migrates,

[1] Lassen supposes that three kinds of gross elemental bodies are here defined, the subtle being only subtle relatively, or in comparison with uterine and other bodies or substances; but the *liṅga* is not formed of the gross elements; it is a compound of the substance of the three internal organs and of the finer elements called *tanmātrāṇi*. All are bodies or developed forms, but not of the same materials.

[2] *Saha prabhūtais*. *Prabhūta*, that which is brought into being, often used with an idea of multitude connected with it; "in grossem Maase vorhanden" (St. Peters. Lex.). Colebrooke has "together with the great elements;" Lassen, "crassa" simply. The reference is not to the gross elements, but to the substances formed from them.

never enjoys, and is endowed with dispositions" (*bhāvās*).

After dividing the elements into two classes—those which have no specific marks and those which have such marks—the Sānkhya philosophy divides the latter into three divisions: (1.) Subtle bodies; (2.) those which are born of father and mother; and (3.) gross substances or inorganic matter. By the first is meant the subtle or rudimental body called *liṅga*, which forms a curious element in the Sānkhya philosophy. It is a kind of "spiritual" body formed from "intellect" (*buddhi*), egoism, the *manas*, and the subtle elements. It always accompanies the soul as an outward covering or form in migrating to another body. It becomes "specific" by the aggregation of the subtle elements, which in themselves are "non-specific" or undiversified. Each *liṅga* is inseparably connected with its appropriate soul, whose minister it is, until it is no longer required. It has a separate existence from the body which is produced in the womb of the mother. The latter dies and has no more distinct existence, but the *liṅga* never dies; it migrates with the soul. It is endowed with a separate vitality of a subtle kind, but still material, for it is formed from elements which proceed from Prakṛiti, but not of the later or grosser development.[1] It is capable, therefore, of

[1] "Let us begin by supposing that we possess a frame, or the rudiments of a frame, connecting us with the invisible universal, which we may call the spiritual body." "Now, each thought that we think is accompanied by certain molecular motions and displacements in the brain, and part of these, let us allow, are in some way stored up in that organ so as to produce what may be termed our material or physical memory. Other parts of these motions are, however, communicated to the spiritual or invisible body, and are there stored up, forming a memory which may be made use of when that body is free to exercise its

rising to the heaven of Indra or to other celestial abodes, though it may descend to the vilest human forms, or even to the bodies of beasts and reptiles. Kapila does not appear to recognise the possibility of the soul existing independent of material conditions until it has been prepared for its solitary but perfect state by a knowledge of the nature of the outer world and its own higher nature.

The *liṅga* was created primevally, or with the first emanations of Nature (*Prakṛiti*). Its period is therefore indefinite.

It is unconfined, *i.e.*, it is not confined to one body; it is capable of passing into any number of bodies or to any region.

It is permanent, continuing to be the attendant of the soul until the latter has attained by knowledge to a perfect liberation from all matter. The *liṅga* is then resolved into Nature again.

It does not enjoy or possess, for it is only the handmaid or minister of the true sovereign, the soul.

It is of a subtle nature, being formed from the primary emanations of Nature, "intellect (*buddhi*) and the rest." Hence it has dispositions or forms of being (*bhāvās*), as virtue and other faculties or powers. As the S. Tattwa Kaumudī explains its nature, it is "through the influence of intellect (*buddhi*) that the whole of the subtle body is affected by dispositions or conditions, in the same manner as a garment is perfumed by contact with a fragrant *champa* flower."[1]

functions" (The Unseen Universe, p. 159.) This "spiritual body" answers to the *liṅga*, which carries into another state of being the feelings and habits of a previous state.

[1] The *Bauhinia variegata* of Linnæus. It is called *koridāra* in the Asiat. Res. (iv. 285); a leguminous plant; "flowers chiefly purplish and rose-coloured, fragrant."

41. "As a painting does not stand without a support or receptacle,[1] nor a shadow without a stake, &c., so the *liṅga* does not exist unsupported, without specific elements."

42. "Formed for the sake of the soul, the *liṅga*, by the connection of means and their results, and by union with the predominant power of Nature, plays its part like a dramatic actor."

It is affirmed in Distich 41 that the *liṅga* cannot exist alone. It needs a support or receptacle, but what kind of support is not clearly defined. Gauḍapāda reads *aviśeshairvina*, "without *unspecific* elements," *i.e.*, the subtle elements of material things (*tanmātra*). The usual reading is "without specific elements," *i.e.*, "without the grosser elements," as the word is usually translated, but here it means, I think, as in Distich 38, specific forms, which are usually of the gross elements. The *liṅga* alone cannot perform any functions; it must be joined to or enveloped in the *liṅga-śarīra* (liṅga-body,[2]) by which it acts. And this body, when

[1] *Nirāśrayam*, without a receptacle, *i.e.*, the *liṅga-śarira*. The support or receptacle for a picture seems to mean a frame in which it may be fixed; but Colebrooke translates the word by "ground," and the authors of the Peters. Dict. interpret the passage by "wie ein Bild ohne Unterlage" (s. v. *āśraya*). Vijnāna Bihkshu (Com. Sānk. Pravachana iii. 9) makes the *liṅga* to be formed of seventeen principles or factors, the "eleven organs, the five subtle elements and *buddhi* (intellect). Self-consciousness or egoism is included in the latter." He explains the support which the *liṅga* requires to be that of the gross body.

[2] The *liṅga* and the *liṅga-śarīra* (liṅga-body) are sometimes confounded; but the *liṅga* is a rudimental substance, sometimes compared to light, and the *liṅga-śarīra* is its vehicle. "When a dead body is burnt by one who knows and can repeat these verses (Smārta-sūtra, x. 18, 11, and x. 14, 7–11) properly, then it is certain the soul (invested

deposited in the maternal womb, is connected with another body produced in the womb of the mother from gross elements.

This distinction between gross and subtle bodies runs through the whole of Hindū philosophy. It is transferred to other worlds. According to the Institutes of Manu, a subtle body envelops the souls of the wicked, that they may suffer the torments of hell.[1]

This subtle body plays many parts as an actor, in order that the destinies of the soul may be fulfilled, either in successive forms of an united existence, or in a final deliverance from matter. Sometimes it dwells in noble, and at other times ignoble forms, according to the virtues or vices of a former life. These vicissitudes are undergone by the agency of a peculiar energy or attribute (*vibhuti*) of Nature, to whom here a presiding power is given. The *liṅga* is the receptacle of the soul, giving it a kind of attributive or conditioned nature by contact, and it bears the soul, which never

with a kind of subtle body) rises along with the smoke to heaven" (Indian Wisdom, p. 206). Professor Williams adds, "The eighth Sūtra of chap. iv. states that a hole ought to be dug north-eastward of the Āhavanīya fire and strewn with the plants Avakā and Śīpāla; and the commentator adds that the soul of the dead man, invested with its vehicular subtle body (called *ātivāhika* and sometimes *adhishṭhāna*, and distinct from the *liṅga* or *sūkshma*, being *angushṭha-mātra*, 'of the size of a thumb'), waits in this hole until the gross body is burnt, and then emerging, is carried with the smoke to heaven."

The Hindū commentators are much perplexed by the word "specific" being applied to the subtle body of the *liṅga*. There is, however, no real inconsistency in the language of Iśwara Kṛishṇa. The subtle body which is the envelope of the *liṅga* is specific or diversified by being formed of diverse elements, though each element is unspecific. On this is based the personality of each individual, for these elements may be combined in various degrees.

[1] Manu, xii. 16. This body is said to be formed of the five gross elements (*mātrāni*), not "(nerves of) five sensations," as Sir C. Haughton translates the word.

acts, from one body to another. It forms the personality of each individual.

43. "Conditions or states of being are transcendental, natural, and modified. These (last) are virtue and the rest. They must be considered as including cause (lit. cause-receptacle), and those which belong to the uterine germ and the rest of the gross body as including (or belonging to) effect."[1]

44. "By virtue an ascent to a higher region is obtained; by vice a descent into a lower. Deliverance is gained by knowledge, and bondage by the contrary."

45. "By the absence (or destruction) of passion there is a dissolution of Nature (*Prakṛiti*[2]) or (the power of Nature is destroyed). Transmi-

[1] Colebrooke's translation is, "Essential dispositions are innate. Incidental, as virtue and the rest, are considered appurtenant to the instrument." The meaning of the distich is that there are conditions or states of being in every specific existence, but that they differ in their nature and their source.

[2] Lassen's translation is, "placiditate deletur potentia naturæ." The original is *vairāgyāt prakṛitilayah* (from the absence of passion is nature-dissolution). The Hindū commentators interpret the words to mean that by dispassion an absorption into Nature is gained, *i.e.*, of the subtle body as well as the gross, but that final deliverance is not hereby gained. So says Vijnāna Bhikshu: "In the absence of knowledge of the distinction (between Soul and Nature), when indifference towards Mind, &c., has resulted from devotion to Nature, then absorption into Nature takes place; for it is declared, 'Through dispassion there is absorption into Nature.' Even through this, *i.e.*, absorption into the cause, the end is not gained, because there is a rising again as in the case of one who has dived" (Comm. on Sānk. Prav., Ballantyne, p. 92). This statement is made because it is a cardinal doctrine of the Sānkhya philosophy that the final liberation of the soul from matter can only be gained by know-

gration is from disorderly passion. By power we gain destruction of obstacles, and the reverse by the contrary."

These conditions or states of being are either innate or constructive (modified). To the former class belong: (1.) The transcendental state (*saṅsiddhika*), obtained only by sages, or, as Gauḍapāda supposes, by the great sage Kapila; (2.) that which is natural (*prākṛitika*), or the state at birth caused by virtue or vice in a previous existence. The constructive or modified condition (*vaikṛitika*) is gained by other means, as by knowledge obtained from a tutor.

The modified conditions are: (1.) Intellectual, as virtue and the rest, *i.e.*, virtue, knowledge, absence of passion, power and their contraries. These conditions have the nature of cause or instrument, for they produce a higher or lower state in a subsequent life, or even final deliverance from matter. (2.) Other superadded conditions belong to the generated body and the progress from infancy to old age. These have only the nature of effect. They are due to external circumstances, and do not produce anything.

By virtue (*dharma*), as a cause, the soul and its subtle body, the *liṅga-śarīra*, may rise to a higher state, either upon earth, or in one of the eight heavens, or supramundane abodes. These are:—

ledge. It does not, however, recognise any absorption of the subtle body into Nature until the soul is entirely free; and hence, notwithstanding the general consensus of Hindū commentators, I think Lassen's translation is correct, and that the meaning is, "By the destruction of passion the influence of the material world (*Prakṛiti*) is destroyed, and the soul is independent, though not yet finally liberated." See Distich 67.

1. The region of the Piśāchas, who are genii of the lowest class.

2 and 3. The regions of the Rākshasas and the Yakshas, of a higher class.

4. That of the Gandharvas, a kind of demigods, the musicians of the higher class of deities.

5. The heaven of Indra (the Sun).

6. That of Soma (the moon).

7. That of the Prajāpatis, the abode of the Pitṛis, or early fathers of mankind, and of the Ṛishis (holy sages).

8. That of Brahmā, the highest heaven.

If, however, the soul is degraded by vice, it may descend to the form of an animal, or it may dwell for a time in the lower regions. Virtue and vice, though not clearly defined, have therefore an influence on the soul's future state, but the final deliverance from matter, when the soul attains to an eternal state of isolated self-existence, can only be obtained by a knowledge of Soul as distinct from Matter. Bondage [1] is the union of the soul with matter, though the matter may be only the subtle body of the *liṅga*, and the place of abode may be the heaven of Brahmā.

By attaining to a complete suppression of passion, it is possible to gain a perfect freedom from the dominion of Nature or the external world, an absolute loosening of the bonds by which the soul is bound to material con-

[1] The bondage that comes from ignorance, according to Vāchaspati, has three degrees: (1.) The bondage of the Materialists, who assume that matter is the whole of being; (2.) of those who consider the soul to be one of the products of Nature (*Prakṛiti*); (3.) of those who, not knowing the nature of the soul, practise moral and religious observances from the hope of gain. These errors confine the soul by an union with a bodily form for various periods. The state of the first is almost hopeless, but the period of bondage for the second class is said to be ten *manwantaras* or 3,084,480,000 years (Wilson, p. 145; St. Hilaire, p. 180). The time of this penance is not, however, quite so long. The *manwantara* is a period of 4,320,000 years.

ditions. The common Hindū interpretation of the passage is, that for a time all the elements which form any envelopment of the soul are absorbed into Nature (*Prakriti*), but they are re-formed again until the soul has gained the knowledge by which alone it can be finally liberated from matter.

Supernatural power may also be gained, and then matter, in all its varied forms, can offer no impediment to the movements of the spiritualised body, which is no longer subject to the laws of the material world; but, on the other hand, there may be a contrary state, in which every obstacle may bar its course.

46. "This is an intellectual production (or evolved state) which is distinguished by the names of obstruction, incapacity, acquiescence (or contentment), and perfection. By the hostile influence (*vimarda*, destruction, ravage, hostile attack) of modal inequalities (or specific differences) the different kinds are fifty."

47. "There are five kinds of obstruction, and, from the imperfection of instruments or organs, twenty-eight of incapacity; acquiescence has nine divisions, and perfection eight."

48. "There are eight divisions of obscurity, and also of illusion; those of extreme illusion are ten; those of gloom and utter darkness are eighteen in each case."

49. "The destructive injuries of the eleven senses, with those of the intellect (*buddhi*), are

accounted as 'incapacity.' The seventeen (injuries) of the intellect are from the opposites of acquiescence and perfection."

50. "Nine varieties of acquiescence are set forth; four internal, named from Nature, means, time, and fortune; five external, relating to abstinence from objects of sense."

The 46th and following distichs form the outline of a Hindū system for "the conduct of the human understanding;" but as they stand, they are too indefinite to have any practical value, and the commentators are not agreed in all points as to the right meaning.

In the phrase "intellectual production" (*pratyaya sarga*). the first part represents *buddhi*, the faculty by which modified sensations are presented as ideas to the gaze of the soul. "By intellectual production," says Professor Wilson, "are to be understood the various accidents of human life occasioned by the operations of the intellect or the exercise of its faculties, virtue, knowledge, impassiveness, and power, or their contraries." It denotes rather new conditions or modifications of the intellect itself, which by the varied action of the modes may be differently formed or modified.[1]

"Obstruction" is explained by Vāchaspati as "ignorance;" by Gauḍapāda as "doubt." It is whatever is opposed to the soul's purpose of final liberation from contact with matter.

Incapacity (*aśakti*) arises from the imperfection of the senses. Acquiescence or contentment (*tushti*) is a passive

[1] Lassen calls the results "mentis conditiones speciales," p. 46.

state of the intellect. Perfection (*siddhi*) means perfect knowledge, not completeness in moral virtue.

The fifty different varieties of these states are defined in the following distichs.

The five kinds of obstruction, according to Gauḍapāda, are obscurity, illusion, extreme illusion, gloom, and utter darkness, which are explained below. The school of Patañjali defines them as ignorance, self-love, love, hatred, and fear. The eight varieties of obscurity correspond, it is said, to the first eight forms of matter. A person may think, for instance, that the soul merges into Nature, intellect, consciousness, or the five rudimental elements, and each of these obscurities or errors obstructs the soul in its efforts for final liberation.

Illusion is defined to be the error which induces men to seek for the eight degrees of supernatural power (see p. 58). The soul is thus drawn aside from its proper aim.

Extreme illusion is the error of seeking happiness in sensual objects, and is interpreted as being tenfold, because gods and men may seek happiness in the pleasures of the senses, and thus there may be a double series of errors arising from the five senses. Thus say all the commentators; but more probably, as M. St. Hilaire has suggested, reference is here made to the five organs of sense and the five organs of action.

Gloom (*tāmisra*) is interpreted "hate," and the explanation is, that a man may hate the ten senses or organs, and the eight degrees of supernatural power. He may thus be as much disturbed and drawn away from his proper aim as by the influence of love. The highest state to which he can attain next to *Nirvāṇa* is one of pure contemplation, in which nothing is hated or loved.

Utter darkness (*andhatāmisra*, lit. the darkness of the blind) is terror. It may be the fear of death in men, and in gods the fear of being expelled from heaven by the Asuras; in each case it is the loss of pleasure or power which is feared; and as their sources are eighteen in number,[1] there are so many varieties of "utter darkness."

The destructive injuries of the eleven organs, *i.e.*, of the organs of sense and action with the *manas*, are deafness, blindness, paralysis, loss of taste and smell, dumbness, mutilation, lameness, constipation, impotence, and insanity. The injuries of the intellect are the inversed or evil forms of acquiescence, of which there are nine varieties, and of perfection, of which there are eight. These states of acquiescence are both internal and external. The internal kind is fourfold. A man may believe, for instance, that Nature does everything and will in time procure the liberation of the soul; he remains, therefore, passive. Or he may rest satisfied with the efficacy of some religious or ascetic observances, or in the idea that liberation will necessarily come in time, or by an accident of fortune.

The five external inversions of acquiescence are abstinence from the five kinds of sensuous pleasure, not from a right idea of their obstructive nature, but merely from a desire to avoid the trouble and anxiety which they may cause by the indulgence of them.

51. "The eight perfections (or means of acquir-

[1] They are, according to Gauḍapāda, the eight sources of supernatural power and the ten objects of perception, or the five objects of sense, twice told, to gods and men. He explains "utter darkness" as profound grief, such as might be felt by one who dies in the midst of all sensual delights.

ing perfection) are reasoning (*ūha*), word or oral instruction (*sabda*), study or reading (*adhyayana*), the suppression of the three kinds of pain, acquisition of friends and liberality (*dāna*). The three fore-mentioned (conditions) are checks to perfection."

The fore-mentioned conditions are the several varieties of obstruction, incapacity, and acquiescence. They are all checks or hindrances in the pursuit of perfect knowledge. Kapila now defines the eight methods or means of attaining it.

Vāchaspati interprets the first source of perfect knowledge, "reasoning," to be "investigation of scriptural authority by dialectics which are not contrary to the scriptures;"[1] but this gloss is evidently due to the Vedāntist views of the commentator. In placing reason as the first source of perfection, Kapila meant to ignore the Vedas, or to place them on a lower scale. Human reason is the highest power which his system acknowledges. It is sufficient to determine what is truth, or at least it is the supreme judge of truth and error, in all that can be known. But its capacity has no defined limits. Such questions as "What am I?" "Whence have I come?" "What is the true purpose of my existence and of all existence?" might be answered, he supposed, by the reason, if not alone, yet as paramount over all other means. But the knowledge gained by reason, though far above virtue, is not man's highest state: it is only a means to the final deliverance of

[1] Wilson, p. 158.

the soul, which will then exist in a state wholly independent, without motion, or consciousness, or knowledge; a state of eternal calmness and repose.

Word (*sabda*) is receiving instruction from a teacher. The suppression of the three kinds of pain (see Distich 1), forms one of the means of acquiring perfection by taking away an obstacle to thought or meditation.

Intercourse with friends is sometimes limited to philosophical discussions with a teacher or fellow-student.

Liberality (*dāna*) is explained as giving money or other offerings to a teacher or to religious devotees; a Brahmanic gloss. Vāchaspati and Nārāyana, however, explain the word as meaning purity (*śuddhi*), deriving it from the root *daip*,[1] to purify, and not from *dā*, to give. M. St. Hilaire approves of this interpretation. Professor Wilson does not reject it. It is, however, contrary both to sound philology and to all we know of Kapila's views of morality. It is due to Patañjali, the author or expounder of the theistic branch of the Sānkhya school. He, however, defines purity to be "undisturbedness of discriminative knowledge through long-continued and uninterrupted practice of veneration." Kapila would have admitted the ultimate point in this definition, but he nowhere speaks of veneration as a means of gaining it, nor did he admit a Supreme Spirit as the object of veneration.

52. "Without dispositions or states of being there would be no *liṅga*, and without the *liṅga* no development or manifestation of conditions (dispositions); whence comes a double creation—one

[1] This root seems to be coined for the occasion. I have not been able to find it in any dictionary, Indian or European.

called personal (of the *liṅga*), and the other conditional (of the dispositions, *bhāvās*)."

In Distichs 40 and 43 it is stated that the *liṅga* migrates, invested with dispositions, according to the conditions of the intellect (*buddhi*), but the effect of these conditions or states of a former being cannot be made manifest except in or by a bodily form, and hence the necessity of the *liṅga*.

The second clause is translated by Colebrooke and Wilson, "Without person there would be no pause (*nirvṛitti*) of dispositions." Wilson explains the passage in his comment on Gauḍapāda's exposition thus: This creation of the *liṅga* is not "indispensable for the existence or exercise of the intellectual conditions or sentiments alone, but is equally necessary for their occasional cessation; thus virtue and vice and the rest necessarily imply and occasion bodily condition; bodily condition is productive of acts of vice and virtue."[1] But here there is no *cessation*, but production of intellectual conditions. Lassen's translation of the passage is, "Nec sine corpusculo conditionum manifestatio;" and in his notes he remarks

[1] Professor Wilson, having failed to perceive the meaning of the passage, has translated incorrectly, I think, the comment of Gauḍapāda: "Without person, without rudimental creation, there would be no pause of dispositions, from the indispensability of virtue and vice for the attainment of either subtle or gross body." I translate the passage thus: "Without the *liṅga*, which is formed of the finer elements (*tanmātrāṇi*), there is no development of dispositions (*bhāvās*), and there would be no beginning of virtue and the rest without a complete formation of subtle and gross body" (na sthūlasukshmadehasādhyatwāddharmāderanaditwāchcha). The soul *per se* knows nothing of virtue or vice. Each is possible only by its union with the subtle body the *liṅga*, and the grosser uterine body. On the other hand, but for the necessity of these conditions there would be no occasion for the *liṅga*.

"*Nirvṛitti* est manifestatio, evolutio, originario vocabuli sensu," referring to Manu i. 31. The translation of the word in the Petersburg Lex. is "fertigwerden," "ausbildung." The meaning of the distich then becomes evident. There is a continual action and reaction of intellectual and personal states, the first causing the latter, and the latter giving manifestation to the former. There is therefore a constant double creation, the *bhāvākhya* (or dispositional) and the *liṅgakya* (of the subtle body, *liṅga*).

Some commentators make the *liṅga* itself to be *buddhi* (intellect) and *bhāvās* to be its conditions. The former interpretation is preferable, for the *liṅga*, though formed of the intellect and other internal organs, is yet something different from them. It is, moreover, conditioned by the state of a former life, which is due to "intellect."

53. "The divine class has eight varieties; the animal,[1] five. Mankind is single in its class. This is, in summary, the world (*sarga*, emanation) of living things."

54. "In the higher world, the quality (or mode) called 'goodness' prevails; below, the creation abounds in 'darkness;' in the midst, 'foulness' or 'passion' abounds. Brahmā and the rest (of the gods) and a stock form the limits."[2]

[1] *Tairyagyonas*, "grovelling" (Colebrooke); "inhumana" (Lassen); "nés de la matrice" (St. Hilaire). The last is certainly wrong, for it would include mankind. The Petersburg Dict. translates it, "standing in relation to beasts" (zu den Thieren in Beziehung stehend), from *tiryaga* (beast) and *yoni* (womb).

[2] Colebrooke's translation is, "In the midst is the predominance of foulness, from Brahmā to a stock;" and Professor Wilson translates Gauḍapāda's commentary thus: "*In the*

The gods are only a created order (*sarga*, emanation). The genii or superhuman beings, such as the Yakshas and Rākshasas, are included in this class. For the eight grades up to Brahmā, see p. 53.

The low or grovelling class has five genera or divisions: (1.) domestic animals (*paśu*); (2.) wild animals, such as deer (*mriga*) and the rest; (3.) birds; (4.) reptiles, including fishes (*sarīsṛipa*); and (5.) fixed things (*sthāvara*), vegetables and minerals.

Man stands alone between these two classes, forming an order by himself. The mode or quality of "goodness" is only, it must be remembered, a light, elastic, etherealised kind of matter, favourable to virtue, but not of a moral nature in itself. Some of the supposed superhuman beings are neither virtuous nor beneficent; on the contrary, they are often evil and malignant. Man is under the influence of the active mode, "passion," and therefore he is miserable. Animals and inanimate things are formed from the mode "darkness;" they are therefore stupid or insensate.

55. "There (in the world of men) the sentient (or intelligent) soul experiences pain arising from old age and death until the *liṅga* has ceased to be; wherefore pain is from the nature of the (*liṅga*)."

midst, in man, *foulness predominates*, although goodness and darkness exist, and hence men for the most part suffer pain. Such is the world, *from Brahmā to a stock*, from Brahmā to immovable things." "In the midst" certainly means in the earth, which is between heaven and the lower regions, and Brahmā does not belong to it, but to the region "above." Gauḍapāda's comment is, "This, *i.e.*, *from Brahmā to a stock*, is equivalent to from Brahmā to immovable (inanimate) things." In the S. Pravachana (iii. 50) it is said, "In the midst" passion "abounds," *i.e.*, as Vijnāna Bhikshu interprets the passage, "in the world of mortals."

Here is the climax of the Sānkhya philosophy, the liberation of the soul from every kind or form of matter, even that of its subtle vehicle the *liṅga*. It is from contact with matter that pain arises. The soul knows nothing of decay or pain in itself, but the *liṅga* is so closely connected with it that it becomes sensible of the imperfections and pains that belong to bodily conditions by this union.[1] But when at length, by full knowledge, the soul escapes from "the body of this death," it knows pain no more; the *liṅga* is then absorbed again in Nature (*Prakṛiti*). Kapila, however, does not say where the soul exists after its final severance from matter.

56. "Thus this (development of being), formed from Nature (*Prakṛiti*), from the great principle (*Buddhi*, intellect) down to specific beings, is for the deliverance of each individual soul. This action (*ārambha*, effort) is for another, as if for itself (Nature)."

57. "As the production of milk, which is unintelligent (unknowing), causes the growth of the calf, so the development[2] of Nature causes the liberation of the soul."

58. "As people engage in acts that they make desires to cease, so does the undeveloped principle (*Prakṛiti*) for the liberation of the soul."

[1] "So long as we are entangled and oppressed by the body, we shall never arrive at the point which we aim at, namely, at truth. The body is a constant enemy to us. The necessity of providing for its wants and the diseases which fall upon it are constant interruptions. It fills us with desires, cravings, fears, delusions, follies" (Plato, Phædo, c. 28).

[2] *Pravṛitti* (flowing forth, emanation) is used in each line.

Kapila here maintains that a purpose or design may be formed and completed unconsciously, without a designing mind. He feels, however, the difficulty of connecting design with unintelligent matter, and adduces as an argument in his favour the fact that in the udder of a cow the milk by which the calf is nourished is secreted without the action of intelligence. This is a favourite illustration among his disciples, and is generally put forward as conclusive on the subject. But the question still remains, is this adaptation the work of an intelligent designer, or the result of blind chance, a fortuitous concourse of atoms only? Kapila does not enter upon an examination of this question. He is content to assume the non-existence of a designer, because the milk is produced, and there is no evidence of a designing mind in the course of its production. He does not ask if the arrangement of the several parts or functions for the attainment of this end were fortuitous or not. In India, however, as in other parts of the world, the idea of a design without an intelligent designer is held to be an impossible assumption. "Whether this (evolution)," says Vāchaspati, "be for its own purpose or that of another, it is a rational principle that acts. Nature cannot act thus without rationality, and therefore there must be a reason which directs Nature. Embodied souls, though rational, cannot direct Nature, as they are ignorant of its character; therefore there is an omniscient Being, the director of Nature, who is Īśwara (Lord[1])." This is sound reasoning, but it was not adopted by Kapila. He saw that there was an adaptation of means to an end in the supply of a suitable

[1] Wilson, p. 168.

nourishment for the calf; but as the cow supplies it without bringing an intelligent agency to bear upon the production, so Nature works in providing what is for the benefit of the soul. She is not acted upon by any external force or necessity, nor is she directed by a superior power, nor does she produce by the necessary action of some internal mechanism, but by a blind instinct, as men act to gratify some desire that rises within them without volition.

59. "As a dancer, having exhibited herself on the stage ceases to dance, so does Nature (*Prakṛiti*) cease (to produce) when she has made herself manifest to soul."

60. "Generous Nature, endowed with modes, causes by manifold means, without benefit to herself, the benefit of Soul, which is devoid of modes, and makes no return."

61. "Nothing is more modest than Nature; that is my judgment. Saying 'I have been seen,' she does not expose herself again to the view of Soul."[1]

62. "Wherefore not any Soul is bound, or is liberated, or migrates. It is Nature, which has many receptacles (or bodily forms of being), which is bound, or is liberated, or migrates."

[1] Lassen's translation of Distich 61 is this: "Procreatrix, pudibundæ instar puellæ, non iterum invisit presentiam Genii, dicens ne hilum quidem est; hæc mihi nascitur persuasio, postquam sum conspecta." It is certainly wrong. The true reading is not *prakṛitih*, which Lassen assumes, but *prakritêh*. Colebrooke's translation is: "Nothing, in my opinion, is more gentle than Nature." It is not, however, gentleness, but modesty, that is attributed to Nature, by which she withdraws from the gaze of the soul.

Beautiful as poetry, but not very philosophic, nor in strict harmony with other parts of the Sānkhya philosophy. Kapila, or Īśwara Kṛishṇa, forgets that Nature (*Prakṛiti*) has no personality, no power of volition, and no consciousness. But the instincts of the soul (if I may use the term) are often too strong for mere reason. Kapila, like others, discards the idea of unconscious matter when he breaks away from the meshes of his false logic, and Nature is endowed with all the qualities that belong to a thinking and self-conscious mind.

Nature is called generous, or not seeking return, because she acts for the benefit of Soul, which, having no modes, cannot act, and therefore can give nothing in return. She exhibits herself to Soul in the forms of gods, men, and animals, and by the properties of sensuous objects, and by showing thus to Soul its own separate nature, provides for its liberation from Matter. When this has been gained, the result is eternal. Soul is never again joined to Matter; and Nature, having shown herself once, retires from the scene, "as a modest matron who may be surprised in dishabille by a strange man, but takes good heed that another shall not behold her off her guard."[1]

It is not the soul, therefore, which is liberated or bound, or which migrates, *i.e.*, it is not liberated or bound in and by itself, nor does it migrate by any act of its own. It is the *liṅga* which migrates, &c.; the soul is merely passive. "These circumstances," says Vāchaspati, "are ascribed to and affect Soul, as the superior, in the same manner that victory and defeat are attributed to and relate to a king, though actually occurring to his generals; for they are his servants, and the gain or loss is his, not

[1] S. Tattwa Kaumudī, Wilson, p. 173.

theirs." The distinction is more than this. Kapila has a lofty idea of the soul. It is incomparably superior to matter. All outward things minister to it, as the servants of a king minister to his desires. But the servants and the king are both of a Hindū type. The servants are mere slaves, without reflection or power of self-action; and the king dwells in solitary grandeur, shutting himself up in his palace, and refusing to share in the ordinary pursuits of mankind, from whom he is separate, living in aimless and unchanging inaction.

63. "Nature by herself binds herself by seven forms; she causes deliverance for the benefit of soul by one form."

The seven forms are virtue, passiveness, power, vice, ignorance, passion, and weakness. The one source of deliverance is knowledge, which when Nature has given, she has accomplished her object and retires.

64. "It is thus that by the study of principles (*tattwa*) the knowledge is obtained which is complete,[1] incontrovertible, and absolute;[2] by which it is said, 'I am not,' 'Nothing is mine,' and 'There is no ego.'"

The meaning of this distich has been variously understood. To M. Cousin it seems to teach "an absolute nihilism, the last fruit of scepticism;" but this idea is contrary to the fundamental principles of the Sānkhya

[1] *Apariśesha*, which leaves nothing remaining, including everything in itself.

[2] *Kēvala*, abstract, the only one science.

philosophy. To Kapila the soul was the most real of all things—self-existent, never born, and never dying. It becomes, by knowledge of the doctrines of Kapila, wholly separate from matter, and this separation is the soul's highest achievement. This is distinctly expressed in the S. Pravachana: "By renunciation through study of principles (it is said), 'It is not thus; it is not thus,'" *i.e.*, the soul is different from all the emanations of Prakṛiti. The Sānkhya Pravachana Bhāshya gives this interpretation: "'Neither I am' denies the agency of soul; 'nor is aught mine' denies attachment (to any objects); 'nor do I exist' denies its appropriation (of faculties);"[1] or, as the Chandrikā explains the last clause, "By this, difference from egotism is expressed." We learn, then, by these testimonies, confirmed by other parts of the Sānkhya system, that the phrase "I am not" (*nasmi*) denies only life in its ordinary form, existence of a moving, acting kind; "naught is mine" implies that the soul has now no adjuncts to itself, it is wholly self-contained; "nor is there an ego" affirms that the soul exists without consciousness or sense of personality. The final and supreme state of the soul is then an abstract, passionless, unconscious state, which is the nearest possible approach to the Buddhist idea of *Nirvāṇa*,[2] which, in its full completeness, is simple annihilation. The last stage of the wise man, according to Buddhism, before absolute extinction of being is gained, is very nearly the final state of the soul in the system of Kapila. But the Sānkhya doctrine maintains the continued existence of soul, though in a perfectly unconditioned and passive state, as an eternal entity.

[1] Wilson, p. 180.
[2] See Professor Childers' Pali Dict., s. v. *Nirvāṇa*.

65. "By this (knowledge), Soul, as a spectator, unmoved and at ease, beholds Nature, which has now reverted from the seven forms (to its primitive state), because the capacity (or desire) of producing has now ceased."

66. "'It has been seen by me,' says the one, ceasing to regard; 'I have been seen,' says the other, and ceases to act. In the (mere) conjunction of the two there is no motive for production."[1]

The soul having gained the supreme knowledge, beholds Nature as a spectator looks upon an actress. The seven forms are described at page 96. There is no longer any occasion for virtue, or for any condition of ordinary life, because the soul has now become entirely independent of Nature. The latter has now also no capacity (*vaśa*) of producing. In the language of Vāchespati, "The two objects of soul, fruition and discrimination, are the excitements to the activity of Nature: if they do not exist, Nature is not stimulated (to production). In the text, the term 'motive' implies that by which Nature is excited to creation (to evolve the existing world), which cannot be in the non-existence of the objects of Soul." Creation, or the development of Nature, does not arise from the union of Soul and Matter, as some other philosophers have taught, but solely from Nature acting to satisfy the needs or the desires of Soul.

All things, however, return to unconsciousness. Con-

[1] St. Hilaire's translation is "Et bien que l'union de tous deux puisse subsister encore," &c. This is incorrect. Soul and matter can never be reunited, according to Kapila, when the soul has been liberated from it. An assertion or theory of others is here denied.

sciousness, or the ego, is a development from *buddhi* (intellect), which proceeds directly from Nature (*Prakṛiti*); but in the consummation of all things this element retires within *buddhi*, and the latter is absorbed again into *Prakṛiti*. Soul and Matter continue to exist, but each in an isolated, independent state.

But if the liberation of the soul is gained by knowledge, how then does the soul remain connected with matter when the requisite knowledge has been obtained? This inquiry is answered in the following distich :—

67. "By the attainment of complete knowledge, virtue and the rest have become no longer a real cause;[1] yet a body continues to be held, as a potter's wheel continues to revolve from the force of the previous impulse."

68. "This separation from body being obtained, when Nature ceases to act because her purpose has been accomplished, then the soul obtains an abstraction from matter[2] which is both complete and eternal."

By perfect knowledge the soul is freed from the influence of virtue and the rest, which are the cause of bodily

[1] Dist. 67. Lassen translates the first line thus: "Postquam consummatæ scientiæ acquisitione invenit genius nullum esse pietatis ceterarumque conditionum usum." The lit. translation is, "By the attainment of complete knowledge, virtue and the rest have become a name-cause (*nāmakāraṇa*)," *i.e.*, a cause only in name. Cf. *nāmayajna* (name-sacrifice), a false or hypocritical sacrifice. Colebrooke has "Virtue and the rest become causeless," which is ambiguous. St. Hilaire, "La vertu et les autres facultés cessent aussitot d'être des causes."

[2] *Kaivalya*, the state of complete abstraction or isolation from matter.

existence in a higher or lower form. But for a time their influence may be felt, as a wheel will continue to revolve after the impulse which caused it to move has ceased. There is no longer any need of the activities of Nature when knowledge has freed the soul from all material conditions, and all things connected with this activity, such as virtue or love, will be known no more. The soul's perfect and final deliverance from the bondage of matter has been gained. No new character can be assumed; no birth into any kind of bodily state, even that of the gods, can follow. The drama of life is ended, and the actors retire from the stage for ever.

69. "This abstruse knowledge, which is for the benefit of the soul, wherein the origin,[1] production (or development)[2] and dissolution of beings are described, has been thoroughly expounded by the great *ṛishi* (Kapila)."

70. "This supreme purifying doctrine the sage compassionately imparted to Asuri; Asuri taught it to Panchaśikha, by whom it was extensively made known."

71. "Handed down by disciples in succession, it has been compendiously written in Áryá metre by the noble-minded Īśwara Kṛishṇa, having fully learned the demonstrated truth."

72. "The subjects treated in seventy distichs are those of the complete science, containing sixty

[1] *Sthiti* is here, I think, the German *dasein*, coming into formal being (see Peters. Dict. s.v.); prim. fixity, place.

[2] *Utpatti*, going forth.

topics, excluding illustrative tales, and omitting also controversial questions."[1]

"Thus is completed the book of the Sānkhya (philosophy), uttered by the venerable, great-minded, and divine Kapila."

"*May prosperity attend it.*"

We have in the preceding distichs an outline, and it is no more than an outline, of the philosophic system taught by Kapila. In what manner or to what extent it was explained by its author we do not know. The comments upon it by Gauḍapāda and others are comparatively modern. It is not certain that they offer an accurate tradition of the manner in which it was expounded by Kapila himself, for some of them are evidently influenced by a desire to make its doctrines accord with the dogmas of the prevalent Vedāntist system. But even as an outline, it is interesting as the first recorded system of philosophy, the first attempt to answer, from human perception and reason alone, the mysterious questions, "What am I?" "From what source have I sprung?" and "For what purpose do I exist?"

The system of Kapila is essentially a philosophy. Practically, as some of our modern philosophers, he had no theology. He admitted, indeed, the existence of gods, but they were only emanations from Prakṛiti

[1] The reference is here to such works as the Sānkhya Pravachana, which consists of six chapters or readings, of which the first three are devoted to an exposition of the Sānkhya system, the fourth contains some short illustrative tales (*ākhyāyikās*), and the fifth offers some arguments against the objections of opposite schools of thought.

(Nature), and are to be absorbed hereafter into this all-comprehending source, as all other forms of material life. He rejects, with evident scorn, the rites which the Vedas assumed or commanded. In his view they were both impure and inefficient. They enjoined sacrifice, which he rejected because it required the shedding of blood, and it could not procure the final liberation of the soul from the bondage of a material connection. Neither religion nor morality could avail to procure this supreme state. It could only be gained by knowledge, nor yet by every kind of knowledge; but only by the Sānkhya philosophy, whereby the soul gains a knowledge of the external world and of its own higher nature.

This was the sole purpose of Kapila's philosophy. He had no desire to raise mankind to a higher degree of moral excellence or a more perfect civilisation, either as a means to provide more amply for the uses or the pleasures of his kind, or to gratify a love of knowledge for its own sake. To him, the world of matter, enfolding and producing so much pain, is to be regarded only as an enemy. Our present physical life is a mere bondage; it is full of pain; it can never be the source of anything but sorrow and degradation.[1] The aim of philosophy is simply to free the soul from this and

[1] Compare the language of Jeremy Bentham: "Nature has placed mankind under the governance of two sovereign masters, pleasure and pain. . . . On the one hand, the standard of right and wrong, on the other, the chain of causes and effects, are fastened to their throne."

"Pain is in itself an evil, and indeed, without exception, the only evil, or the words good and evil have no meaning" (Introduction to Principles of Morals, i. 1, and x. 9).

Kapila, like Schopenhauer, goes, however, farther than Bentham; for his is a system of Pessimism, though older than the German by more than two thousand years. Life, *i.e.*, conscious life, not merely contains evil: it is an unmixed evil. The better state, nay, the best of all, is the un-

every other connection with matter for ever. We must seek to cast it away, as men cast off a vile and loathsome garment; and this emancipation must be gained by the soul itself, without the aid—if such aid can be obtained—of any external power or influence.

Kapila saw the necessity, in any system of philosophy, of an examination into the sources of our knowledge. If these cannot be defined accurately, or if their information cannot be relied upon, it is evident that there cannot be any philosophy, for there can be no certain knowledge. He admitted three such sources: (1.) The perceptions of outward things gained from the senses; (2.) the logical faculty or reason of man, by which inferences may be drawn from that which is directly known to other truths which are enfolded in this knowledge, but are not perceptible in themselves; (3.) valid testimony. The senses can only inform us of specific objects, but he accepted our sense-perceptions as representing a real external world, which exists in itself, and not merely as a projection of our sensations or thoughts. The Vedāntist doctrine, that the material world is only *māyā*, or illusion, was not held by him; it was, in fact, a speculation of a much later date. Kapila admitted the truth of the perceptions which we receive from the senses, but he saw that their extent is limited by various causes, and that many things do and must exist of which they cannot give us any direct information. Here then the logical faculty begins to work. We may reason either *a priori* from cause

conscious impassive life, in which all things were before the evil birth of reason and consciousness. The highest aim of both systems is not self-sacrifice, but *self-suppression*, the annihilation of the conscious self, which is the cardinal principle of Buddhism.

to effect, or *a posteriori* from effect to cause, or by analogy. The relation of cause and effect is real and necessary; but causation is not properly a creation of anything—it is only an emanating force: the effect existed fully beforehand in the cause,[1] of which it is only a development or issue, as a stream emanates from, and is thus created by, the fountain from which it springs. In the system of Kapila, a pure creation is impossible. Each individual soul and every particle of matter has existed from all eternity. Nor can either perish. They *must* exist for ever; the soul in an unconditioned, unchanging, isolated state; and matter, including therein intellect and consciousness, will be absorbed for ever in Nature (*Prakṛiti*).

We may also reason by analogy, or, as Sir. W. Hamilton terms it, "philosophical presumption,"[2] which Kapila perceived to be "a natural or ultimate principle of intelligence." How Kapila explained and defended this method of proof we do not know. The opinions of his commentators have been already explained (see page 22).

Beyond this range some things are known by "valid testimony." Under what conditions or for what purposes testimony is "valid" we are not informed. Nor do we know whether Kapila admitted what is called *śruti*, or revelation, as coming within this definition. His followers

[1] "When we are aware of something that begins to be, we are, by the necessity of our intelligence, constrained to believe that it has a cause. But what does the expression *that it has a cause* signify? If we analyse our thought, we shall find that it simply means, that as we cannot conceive any new existence to commence, therefore all that now is seen to arise under a new appearance had previously an existence under a prior form. . . . We think the causes to contain all that is contained in the effect; the effect to contain nothing which was not contained in the causes" (Hamilton, Lect. on Metaph., ii. 377).

[2] Lectures on Logic, ii. 166.

gave a modified assent to the Vedas (*śruti*), and also to the teaching of tradition (*smṛiti*), that is, of the ancient sages as handed down to posterity orally or by writings; but the highest position, the sole emancipating power, was given to Kapila's system of philosophy, which could work out deliverance for the soul without the aid of the Vedas,[1] either in their dogmatic or ritual teaching.

It is by the logical faculty we attain to the knowledge of Nature (*Prakṛiti*); the oneness from which all material forms have been developed.[2] It is itself the Undeveloped (*avyakta*); eternal, and, in its essence, unalterable. All material existences are only developed modes of the One. In like manner, some of the Greek philosophers inferred, as a necessity of thought, that the many forms of sensible objects must be referred to one primeval substance as their source. They affirmed, as Kapila, that this was not one of the gross elements, as fire or water, but an invisible, universal, and formless substance (*ἀνόρατον εἶδος τι καὶ ἄμορφον πανδεχές.*)[3] But they maintained either that

[1] "The Vedānta maintained that the acquisition of truth is independent of caste or any other distinction, and that the highest knowledge, which is the chief end of man, cannot be imparted by the Vedas (*vide* Katha, ii. 23); yet it insisted that a knowledge of the Vedas was necessary to prepare the mind for the highest knowledge. This the Sānkhya denied altogether, and though it referred to the Vedas, and especially to the Upanishads, still it did so only when they accorded with its own doctrines, and it rejected their authority in a case of discrepancy" (Dr. Röer, Introd. to Svetaśvatara Upanishad, p. 36).

[2] The *Prakṛiti* of Kapila answers to the *Wille* of Schopenhauer. It is a blind unconscious force, or rather a primal substance, with a potentiality of force through the constituent called passion or foulness, out of which conscious life was an unhappy development.

[3] Plato, Timæus: "This mother and receptacle of all visible and sensible things we do not call earth, nor air, nor fire, nor water, nor anything produced from them, or from which these are produced. It is an invisible and formless thing, the recipient of everything (all-embracing), participating in a certain way of the intelligible, but in a way very difficult to seize."

this first principle was God, as the Eleatics, or that it was fashioned by an Intelligence superior to this primeval substance, and independent of it. In the system of Kapila no place is found for the plastic hand of an intellectual Power in the formation of the world. The one primeval source was simply Matter, and in all its developments was wholly unconnected with the working of Mind. It wrought, and for a distinct purpose, but unconsciously, and by a "potentiality" which dwelt entirely within itself.

How then did Nature (*Prakṛiti*) begin to work? Because, says Kapila, though formless, it has modes or constituents of its being. When these are in a state of equipose, Nature is at rest. When the equipose is disturbed, then Nature begins to work. The impelling influence was an unconscious purpose to free the souls of men from all contact with matter, which is the source of pain. For this purpose it first sent forth intellect (*buddhi*), the first-born of all created things. But the nature and functions of this first product are not clearly defined. It has a faculty of ascertainment; and by this Kapila means a determinant power by which the perceptions of sense-objects are defined in an ultimate form, that the soul may look upon them and gain a knowledge of their nature. From intellect (*buddhi*) consciousness or egoism is evolved. It is from this product of thought that a knowledge of the difference between subject and object is gained. But consciousness, in emanating from intellect, becomes a separate entity, and the intellect works without any consciousness of its working or of its effects. From egoism or consciousness, *i.e.*, conscious mind-matter,[1] spring the *manas* (mind), the ten organs of sense and action, and the five subtle elements (see page 18). The *manas* is an internal faculty, the doorkeeper of the senses, which are the doors through which the soul gains a knowledge of Nature. It receives the sensations which the senses give from outward things, and has a formative power. Our sensations hereby become perceptions, and these, passed on to consciousness, become individualised as "mine;" then by the intellect these individualised perceptions become, in the language of Sir W. Hamilton, "concepts or judgments," and are fit to be presented to the soul.[2] This is as near an approximation to the ideology of Kapila as we can offer in terms derived from another system. It is not an exact representation,

[1] "Mind is the one ultimate reality; not mind, as we know it, in the complex forms of conscious feeling and thought, but the simpler elements out of which thought and feeling are built up. The hypothetical ultimate element of mind, or atom of *mind-stuff*, precisely corresponds to the hypothetical atom of matter, being the ultimate fact of which the material atom is the phenomenon. Matter and the sensible universe are the relations between particular organisms, that is, mind organised into consciousness and the rest of the world. This leads to results which would, in a loose and popular sense, be called Materialist. But the theory must, as a metaphysical theory, be reckoned on the Idealist side. To speak technically, it is an Idealist monism" (Art. on Prof. Clifford, Fort. Rev., May 1879). This *mind-stuff* of Professor Clifford's theory corresponds to the *ahaṅkāra* of Kapila, from which the visible universe has been developed. But Kapila supposed *ahaṅkāra* to be developed from *Prakṛiti* (primal matter), and taught the existence of Soul as the true cognitive power.

[2] The process in the formation of ideas and of the resulting action, as taught by Kapila, is not very different from the conclusions of our modern savants. Wundt thus defines the several steps of the process:—"1. The transition from the organ of sense to the brain (the *manas* of Kapila); 2. The entrance into the field of view of consciousness or perception (egotism); 3. The entrance into the point of view of attention or apperception (*buddhi* or intellect); 4. The action of the will in giving the necessary impetus to the motor nerves; 5. The transmission of this motor excitation to the muscles" (the action of the soul in directing by volition). (Grundzüge, der physiol. Psychologie, Leipsic, 1873–74.)

nor have we a phraseology which will suffice for this purpose; for, in Kapila's system, the "mind" (*manas*), consciousness, and "intellect" (*buddhi*) are all only forms of developed matter. The "intellect" has no proper cognition, though from its proximity to soul this is sometimes ascribed to it. Hence the common Hindū saying, "Agency from affection, intelligence from proximity," *i.e.*, the apparent agency of the soul, which never acts, is from the affection or influence of *buddhi*, and the apparent intelligence of *buddhi* is from its proximity to soul.

The *manas* is classed with the ten organs of sense and action from its immediate connection with them. These organs and the *manas*, together with the five subtle elements out of which the five gross elements are formed, sprang directly from consciousness. Here we seem to have a glimpse of the Hegelian theory that Thought and Being are one absolutely; subject and object,[1] which appear to be contradictory to each other, being really one, and existence the relation of the two. Perhaps we may say that it is nearer the doctrine of Schelling, that subject and object are really distinct from each other, but yet only the manifestation of the absolute essence in different stages of development. This absolute essence may be supposed to be thought or matter, and thus we have the system of the Idealists and that of the Materialistic school. "If the subject be taken as the original and genetic, and the object evolved from it as its product, the theory of Idealism is established. On the other hand, if the object be assumed as the original and genetic, and the subject evolved from it as its product, the theory of Materialism

[1] Morell, Hist. of Mod. Phil., ii. 168.

is established."[1] The system of Kapila does not, however, quite accord with this definition. Here the subjective element is genetic, but it is not ideal or spiritual. It is itself only a development of a material nature. As far, then, as the outward world and the inner life of consciousness are concerned, Kapila is a Materialist; but not wholly so. The soul exists apart from both, but it never creates, nay, it never acts. It exists simply as light, self-contained and eternally distinct.

In the evolution of the five gross elements from the five subtle forms or elements of matter, and in the general process by which all existing forms have been produced, we have, in a crude form, the doctrine of development; but it is a development, not from a lower to a higher state of being, but from a higher or more subtle state to one more gross, and, therefore, more adapted to the senses. Kapila seems to have had a dim apprehension of the fact that the gross elements or forms of matter are not ulti-

[1] Hamilton, Metaphysics, i. 297. There are some points of contact between the system of Fichte and that of Kapila which deserve notice. Fichte contends that the absolute Ego, the I by myself I, must be something different from consciousness, for this is only a certain state of the real Ego. It is the Ego "affirming itself." With this absolute Ego, distinct from consciousness, the Purusha (person) or soul of Kapila agrees. But the Ego, in affirming itself, is also conscious of the non-Ego, or is determined by the necessary law of its nature, and "distinguishes between itself as a definite representation and everything else which is not that representation; it only comes to know itself perfectly by that contrast." So Kapila taught that soul only knows itself by knowing Prakṛiti (Nature). Further, Fichte maintained that we have no knowledge—and his work is the "Doctrine of *Science*"—of the non-Ego except by concepts or representations which are due, in part, to the mind, and, so far, are created by it. The mind or Absolute Ego, which is an intuitive principle, as with Kapila, thus sees only what in part it has formed. Kapila expressed a similar thought by teaching that from consciousness all the subtle and gross forms of matter emanate, but this consciousness is clumsily represented as distinct from soul, because the latter cannot act.

mate forms, as the Greek philosophers generally supposed them to be; but as a scientific analysis had not yet showed how to resolve any of these forms into more primitive elements, no more can be claimed for Kapila than the invention of a fanciful hypothesis which modern science has shown to have a limited substratum of truth.

All these productions are only mode-developments of Nature (*Prakṛiti*). They vary in their kind, as these several modes or constituent elements of Nature are compounded in them, or as one or the other may be the predominant quality. But all these effects are one in their source, in which they were virtually contained, for an effect is only the cause in a state of development. "Ex nihilo nihil fit" was an axiom in Hindū philosophy long before it was expressed in the schools of Europe. Hence Nature, the all-embracing, never had an origin. It is, like the soul, eternal and self-subsisting.[1]

The psychology of Kapila is entirely Oriental in the base of its conception. The soul is a monarch superior to Nature, which ministers to it, but a monarch of an Eastern kind. It dwells apart in a lofty but barren isolation. The soul alone *sees*, *i.e.*, has a true cognition

[1] It is curious that the latest philosophy—Von Hartmann's Philosophy of the Unconscious—should accord in many points with its earliest development in the system of Kapila. 1. In each system the source of all existing forms is an unconscious Monism, which is self-existent. 2. The unconscious first principle develops consciousness. 3. In this conscious life only misery can prevail. 4. Pain is a necessary consequence of the normal development of the first principle, and must remain as long as the present system continues. 5. The ideal state, for which we are to labour and wait, is an unconditioned, unconscious state, the *nirvāṇa* of the Buddhist school. 6. Virtue and vice are only accidents of material conditions. The great aim of life is not to attain to goodness or even a high intellectual state, but only deliverance from pain, which is the chief, if not the only evil. (See Note D.)

of things. It can behold and understand Nature. By this knowledge the soul knows itself, and in knowing itself it gains an eternal liberation from Nature, and therefore from pain. The soul then gains its supreme state of unmoving, unconscious self-existence, which it never afterwards loses. Until this state has been gained, it is enveloped in a body formed from the subtle elements of Nature, the *liṅga* or *liṅga śarīra*, which is affected by the modes of Nature, and is fated to migrate into bodies of a higher or lower state until the soul becomes entirely free. The *liṅga* enters into the womb, and forms the inner frame over which the bodily form derived from the mother is gradually wrought. This latter body perishes entirely in death, but the *liṅga* survives until the soul, by knowledge, becomes prepared for a separate life, and then it is absorbed into the universal Nature from which it sprung.

This theory of the *liṅga* deserves more consideration than it has received from either ancient or modern expounders of the Sānkhya philosophy. It plays an important part in what we must call, though improperly, the moral element of the system. It is the seat of those dispositions, whether moral or physical, which in the Western systems are generally referred, so far as they are moral, to the soul. But Kapila attributes to the soul only a passive state, and to the *liṅga*, which is formed from the substance of the internal organs and the subtle forms of matter, is assigned the congeries of states or affections which form the individuality of each separate being. "The commentators agree," says Professor Wilson (page 130), "that subtle body (the *liṅga*) is subject to enjoyment or suffering only through its connection with generated body, understanding apparently thereby, not its abstract capability of either, but the actual condition in which it partakes of them; for it is repeatedly declared that the seat of enjoyment or suffering is *buddhi* or 'intellect,' through the presence of which, as an ingredient in subtle body, it is immediately added, the latter is invested with dispositions (*bhāvas*), that is, with the properties of intellect enumerated in v. 43, virtue, vice, knowledge, ignorance, &c." This is not strictly correct. The "intellect" (*buddhi*) cannot properly be said to enjoy or suffer. The *liṅga* may be called the "acting soul;" it is the "annexe" of the soul, in the language of M. St. Hilaire, and the seat of those qualities by which an individual is formed, and thinks and feels according to his nature. In being compounded of *buddhi* and other substances, it shows what Professor Jowett has called "the interpenetration of the intellectual and moral faculties" (Plato, i. 464).

The grandeur of the soul, in Kapila's system, is unreal and useless. It has no moral elevation. It knows nothing of virtue and vice as connected with itself. It has no purpose beyond itself. It directs in some undefined degree, but it never condescends to work, either for itself or for others. It has no sympathy. Its highest state is one of perfect abstraction from matter and from other souls; a self-contained life, wherein no breath of emotion ever breaks in on the placid surface. The system of Kapila tends then to destroy morality as an active agency against evil; nay, more, it levels so nearly the barrier between virtue and vice, that the difference becomes unimportant except as a matter of sensation. They are, in fact, pleasure and pain, which are both to be avoided; for both imply action, and all action, if not an evil, is at least an imperfection. The true philosopher rises above virtue or vice by his knowledge. He has reached a higher region in which all voluntary action has ceased, and only contemplation remains. But the soul not only rises above all moral influences; it is never in itself either virtuous or wicked. Virtue and vice are conditions of the *liṅga* or spiritual body, as it may be affected by the three modes of Nature. They do not belong to the soul, but are only the results of material conditions. The modes of Nature, which are called "goodness," "foulness," and "darkness," are only the formative elements of Nature, differing indeed in kind, but not good or bad in our European estimate of goodness and badness. They do not affect the soul. The mode or constituent element called "goodness" is the most subtle of all. It is elastic, and has an enlightening or alleviating influence. It is prevalent, therefore, in fire. The mode called "foulness" or "passion" is the emotional element, causing work, and is the source of all pain. The mode called "darkness" is heavy and destructive. It is the cause of stupidity and illusion. Such theories are only the subjective devices of a man who, having observed the manifold differences in the things around him, endeavours to account for them by the assumption of a difference in the constituent elements of the Nature from which, in his opinion, all had primarily issued.

There is no place for duty, or a sense of sin in failing to fulfil it, in the system of Kapila. These are impossible except in connection with a law which proceeds from a source higher than man, and which he is bound to obey. It is singular that Kapila stands so far apart from the rest of his countrymen in ignoring that sense of moral evil which has so deep a root in the Hindū mind. But he is not alone in this. Our modern philosophers decry or ignore those deep, irrepressible instincts of the human heart which in all ages have led to many austere rites for the putting away this sense of moral guilt which presses so heavily on the conscience. They ignore what they do not understand, and for which their systems afford no remedy. But logically Kapila was consistent in rejecting both the idea of duty and of guilt from his system. He did not admit that any Power existed that was of right the ruler of the world,[1] or of any superintending Providence. The soul is sufficient for itself. There is no real, absolute duty, except perhaps that of acquiring knowledge and of gaining thus deliverance from all contact with matter. But this is rather a privilege of the few than a duty incumbent on all. By not obtaining it the soul is doomed to reappear in some new bodily form, but there is no guilt incurred. All actions are not indeed alike; they differ in their power of affecting the conditions of the new life, and may, in this sense, be called good or bad;[2] but the highest degree of virtue is

[1] As Fichte maintained that since the soul can know nothing higher than, or beyond, its own concepts, and therefore the being of a God cannot be proved as a part of science, so Kapila taught that the soul can only know what is presented to it by *buddhi* (intellect), and therefore cannot know absolutely that there is an Īśwara or Supreme Lord of all things, for this idea cannot be thus presented.

[2] Our modern philosophers go further. Some make virtue to be merely a name for a collective sense during many generations of what is useful to mankind. A virtuous action and a fountain of water do not differ in kind. But the latest theory makes it to denote only a healthy and vigorous organisation. "If I have evolved myself out of something like an amphioxus, it is clear that I have become *better* by the change. I have risen in the organic scale; I have become more organic. Of all the changes which I have undergone, the greater part must

in itself unable to procure full deliverance for the soul. Virtue and vice are only conditions of the material envelope of the soul, which knows nothing of either in itself, for it never acts. Knowledge is the only ark by which it can attain to its final position of pure abstraction; but by this ark even the worst might pass over the ocean of this restless world to the haven of perfect and eternal rest.

As the system of Kapila ignored a Supreme Being, it sought only to guide and strengthen man by his own unaided power. It did not, however, address itself to all classes of men alike, though it did not leave the lowest wholly without hope. Even Śūdras and women might possibly hear some one explain this philosophic system, and might receive some benefit from the knowledge thus gained, but it was not addressed primarily to them. It was essentially an esoteric system, designed chiefly for those more instructed or more intelligent classes who could rise to so great a height of philosophic knowledge as the system of Kapila, when perfectly understood, would enable them to reach. It was practically opposed to religious observances, and prayer became a superfluous

have been changes in the organic direction; some in the opposite direction, some perhaps neutral. But if I could only find out which, I should say that those changes which have tended in the direction of greater organisation were good, and those which tended in the opposite direction bad. Here there is no room for proof; the words 'good' and 'bad' belong to the practical reason, and if they are defined, it is by pure choice. I choose that definition of them which must, on the whole, cause those people who act upon it to be selected for survival. The good action, then, is a mode of action which distinguishes organic from inorganic things, and which makes an organic thing more organic" (Prof. Clifford, Nineteenth Century, October 1877). So Kapila taught that goodness was only a material condition, and led only to a happier bodily life.

act, because knowledge could alone accomplish more for the soul than these religious rites; but on this account it did not commend itself to the people of India. It was therefore supplemented and made more popular by Patañjali, of whom, however, little is known. He probably lived about 200 years B.C.; but almost all that we know of him is that he is reputed to be the author of a book called the "Yoga Sūtra," in which the theistic form or modification of Kapila's system is expounded.

The modifications which Patanjali made in this system are not many in number, but they are important both in themselves and in their bearing upon the inner and outer life of mankind. They were mainly (1.) the doctrine of a Supreme Spirit, who directed and presided over the workings of Nature (*Prakṛiti*); and (2.) the enjoining of *yoga*, *i.e.*, the concentration of the soul on the Supreme Being by abstract meditation as the means of obtaining finally *Nirvāṇa*, or absorption into the Divine Essence.[1] Hence this system is called the *Seśwara* or Theistical Sānkhya, and Kapila's the *Nirīśwara* or Atheistical; a term which may also be applied to Buddhism, which apparently owed its origin to the system of Kapila.

"God" (Īśwara, the supreme Ruler), according to Patanjali, "is a soul or spirit distinct from other souls, unaffected by the ills with which all men are beset, unconnected with good or bad deeds and their consequences. In him is an absolute omniscience. He is the instructor of the earliest beings that have a beginning (the deities of the Hindū mythology), himself infinite, unlimited by

[1] In the full attainment of *yoga*, or a mystic union with the Deity, all the affections and the senses are either wholly overcome and destroyed, or they act only as far as necessity requires.

time."[1] Here is an essential difference between the master and his pupil; for Kapila taught that the existence of thought or instruction is dependent on Consciousness, not upon Īśwara, and Consciousness is from the great principle, Buddhi (Intellect).

The means of attaining to Yoga are (1.) *Yama*, self-restraint; (2.) *Niyama*, necessary religious duties; (3.) *Āsana*, postures;[2] (4.) *Prāṇā-yāma*, restraint of breath; (5.) *Pratyāhāra*, subjugation of the senses; (6.) *Dhārāṇa*, fixed control; (7.) *Dhyāna*, contemplation; (8.) *Samādhi*, pious meditation. The aim of the *Yogī* or devotee under this system is to destroy all movement and all thought, that the soul may be absorbed in passive meditation. But as all cannot rise to this elevation, various means of subduing the senses by severe ascetic rites are set forth and commended, and a frequent repetition of the mystic syllable OM is enjoined. By these means the Yogī might attain to a state called *vidēha* (incorporeal) or *kēvala* (abstracted or purely spiritual). In such conditions he is endowed with supernatural wisdom and power. He can enter into the body of another, and even into his mind, and thus may read his thoughts. The attracting power of the earth cannot bind him. He can soar in the air as if carried up by a balloon. He can understand all mysteries of this world and of other worlds. Both the past and the future may lie distinctly before his view. In short, there is no marvel of modern spiritualism that was not equalled, and even surpassed, in India, according to the Yoga system and the popular belief, two thousand years ago.

[1] Yoga-Śāstra, i. 23, 24, 26–29; Colebrooke, i. 264.
[2] Bhagavad Gītā, vi. 13.

Practically the system of Patanjali, though setting forth a very sublime aim, has resulted in the practice of cruel and degrading rites, of almost incredible devices for self-torture, which have no high or purifying purpose, but, on the contrary, often conceal a base and even sensual life. The Yogī is frequently regarded as a mere sorcerer, and in this character he appears in many an Indian drama and popular tale.

SUPPLEMENTARY NOTICE

OF THE

NYĀYA AND VAIŚESHIKA SYSTEMS.

THESE systems are generally classed together, for they agree upon the subjects of which they treat in common, but are distinct in their chief purpose. The Nyāya is not properly a system of philosophy, but an introduction to all such systems, for it treats mainly of the objects and the laws of thought. The Vaiśeshika system is a system of physical science as taught by Kaṇāda, the reputed author of the Vaiśeshika-Sūtra, in which this system is explained. From the singular absence or deficiency of historical data in India, little is known of Gotama or Gautama, the author of the Nyāya, or of Kaṇāda. The former has become the subject of fanciful legend almost to the same degree as Kapila, the author of the Sānkhya system. He is said to have been born in Northern India at the beginning of the Treta Yuga, or second age of the world, and to have married Ahalyā, the daughter of Brahmā. We can only infer from these statements that he was probably a Brāhman, and may have been of noble descent. He is the Aristotle of India, and his Sūtras have always been a popular study among the Hindūs, whose acuteness finds a suitable field in the discussion of dialectic subtleties. A large number of commentators have explained and commented on the system of Gotama, in order to adapt it to popular use.

It is set forth in a treatise called the Nyāya Sūtra, which comprises five divisions or readings, each containing two lessons. These are divided into sections or *prakaraṇas*, relating to distinct topics. In practice, this system is commonly combined with that of Kaṇāda, as in the *Bhāshā-parichchheda*, the popular text-book in India. It is not always easy to distinguish, in the modern schools, what belongs to each system. Both Gotama and Kaṇāda observe the following order in discussion: (1.) enunciation (*uddeśa*); (2.) definition (*lakshaṇa*); and (3.) investigation (*parīkshā*). Enunciation declares by name the subject to be discussed. Definition is the defining of the subject by its peculiar properties or differentiæ. Investigation is an examination of the subject with regard to its peculiar properties.

The first reading or division of the Nyāya Sūtra consists of sixty aphorisms, and the first Sūtra gives a list of the subjects to be discussed. These are sixteen in number: (1.) *Pramāṇa*, or the means by which a right knowledge may be gained; (2.) *Prameya*, or the objects of thought; (3.) *Doubt*; (4.) *Motive*; (5.) *Instance*, or example; (6.) *Dogma*, or determinate truth; (7.) *Argument*, or syllogism; (8.) *Confutation*; (9.) *Ascertainment*; (10.) *Controversy*; (11.) *Jangling*; (12.) *Objection*, or cavilling; (13.) *Fallacy*; (14.) *Perversion*; (15.) *Futility*; and (16.) *Conclusion*, or the confounding of an adversary. Of these, the first two are the chief; the others being only subsidiary, as indicating the course which a discussion may take, from the setting forth of a doubt to the final confutation of the doubter.

Proof or evidence (*pramāṇa*) is of four kinds: (1.)

Pratyaksha, or perception by the senses; (2.) *Anumāna*, inference, which is of three kinds—from cause to effect, from effect to cause, and by analogy; (3.) *Upamāna*, or comparison; and (4.) *Śabda*, word or verbal authority, including revelation and tradition.

Cause (*Kāraṇa*) is defined as that which necessarily precedes an effect, which without the cause could not be; for the relation of cause and effect, connection (*sambandha*), must be considered. This is twofold, implying either simple conjunction (*samyoga*), or intimate and constant relation (*samavāya*),[1] wherein two things must always be joined, as cloth and the threads of yarn which form it. Hence cause is considered as (1.) intimate or direct, as clay is the material cause of pottery, and yarn of cloth; (2.) mediate or indirect, proximate to the intimate cause, as the weaving of yarn in forming cloth; and (3.) instrumental or concomitant, as the loom. In desire, the soul is the direct or intimate cause; the mediate is the conjunction of the soul and its internal organ, the *manas;* the instrumental is knowledge. We may rather call them the aggregate of conditions necessary for the forming either of a material product or a psychical state.

The objects of which a right knowledge may be gained are (1.) soul; (2.) body; (3.) the senses; (4.) the objects of sense; (5.) intellect (*buddhi*); (6.) mind (*manas*); (7.) production, oral, mental, or corporeal; (8.) fault or wrong (*dosha*); (9.) transmigration; (10.) fruit or retribution; (11.) pain; (12.) deliverance, or emancipation.

The soul is different, or individual, in each person, separate from the body and the senses, the seat of knowledge and feeling. It is eternal in duration. Knowledge,

[1] Tarka Sangraha, p. 22; Colebrooke, i. 287.

desire, aversion, volition, pain, and pleasure, imply the existence of soul, which is called a substance, as being the substratum or entity in which these several qualities reside. The soul experiences the fruit or retribution of deeds, good or bad.

The Supreme Soul (*Paramātman*) is One, the seat of eternal knowledge, the maker or former of all things.

Body is the seat of effort and of the organs of sensation. By association with it the soul has fruition, or the feeling of pleasure and pain. It is earthly, for the properties of earth are perceived in it, as solidity, smell, &c. Some supposed the body to be formed of three elements—earth, water, and light or heat; others that it was formed of four, adding air to the former elements. But Gotama rejects these suppositions, mainly on the ground that there is no intimate, absolute union of heterogeneous substances; an argument which Kapila had employed. The distinct kinds, as classified by Vaiśeshika writers are (1.) ungenerated, as those of gods and demigods; (2.) uterine or viviparous; (3.) oviparous; (4.) engendered in filth; and (5.) vegetative or germinating.

The five external organs are not modifications of consciousness, as the Sānkhya philosophy teaches, but are formed of gross matter, earth, water, light, air, and ether, corresponding to the senses of smell, taste, sight, touch, and hearing. There is a sixth sense, an internal organ, *manas* or "mind," which is the organ of the bodily senses. By union with the external senses it produces knowledge of exterior objects. Its office is to separate the sensations, and to present them singly to the soul; and hence it is that the soul does not receive more than one sensation, or rather perception, at the same instant. The *manas* is minutely small, as an atom; for otherwise it might come into connection with many things or many sensations at one time. It is eternal, and distinct from both soul and body.

The objects of sense are odour, taste, colour, feeling, and sound. Under this head are placed the six categories (*padārtha*) of Kaṇāda, which are substance, quality, action, generality or community of properties, particularity or specific quality, and co-inherence or perpetual and intimate relation. Later writers added a seventh, privation or negation.

Intellect is twofold, including notion and remembrance. It is defined as that which manifests or makes known. Its relation to the *manas* is not clearly explained. A notion or concept is either right or wrong. A right notion is that which is derived from a clear proof, and is fourfold: (1.) From perception, as a jar perceived by the bodily organs; (2.) from inference, as fire is inferred from smoke; (3.) from comparison, by which we have a knowledge of genera; and (4.) from revelation, as the notion of celestial happiness, which we have from the Vedas.

A wrong notion is one which is not derived from proof, and is threefold in origin: (1.) From doubt; (2.) false premisses; and (3.) error, as the mistaking of mother-of-pearl for silver.

Remembrance is also either right or wrong. A waking remembrance may be either, but in sleep it is wrong.

Production is the cause of virtue and vice, of merit and demerit. It is oral, mental, or corporeal; speech being considered to be of a compound nature, but does not include unconscious vital functions. It is the result of the three *faults*—passion or extreme desire, aversion or loathing, and error or delusion. The wise man, according to Gotama, is one that avoids these faults, and is profoundly indifferent to all action.

The only motive to action is the desire of attaining pleasure or of avoiding pain.[1]

Transmigration is the passing of the soul to successive bodies.

Blessedness is deliverance from pain. Pain is the primary evil, but there are twenty-one varieties of evil which are the causes of pain, and these are in the organs of sense, the objects of sense, the mental apprehensions, and even in pleasure, for this may be evil and a source of pain, as honey drugged with poison is fatal. The soul attains to this deliverance by knowledge, by meditating on itself, by not earning fresh merit or demerit through actions sprung from desire, and by becoming free from passion through knowledge of the evil inherent in objects. It is knowledge, as in the Sānkhya system, and not virtue, which obtains final deliverance from the body.[2] The latter can only procure a better state of bodily connection; it cannot destroy it.

[1] "A motive is substantially nothing more than pleasure or pain operating in a certain manner.

"Now, pleasure is in itself a good—nay, even setting aside immunity from pain, the only good. Pain is in itself an evil; and indeed, without exception, the only evil, or else the words good and evil have no meaning. And this is alike true of every sort of pain and every sort of pleasure. It follows, therefore, immediately and incontestably, there is no such thing as any sort of motive that is in itself a bad one."

"Nature has placed mankind under the governance of two sovereign masters, *pain* and *pleasure*. It is for them alone to point out what we ought to do, as well as to determine what we shall do" (Jeremy Bentham, Introd. to Prin. of Morals, &c., c. x. ss. 9, 10, c. i. s. 1).

[2] In the system of Bentham there is no more room for virtue, goodness, justice, or unselfish liberality than in the system of Gotama. The base of what is called in these systems morality (a real morality in such systems is impossible) is only the gratifying of desire.

The other subjects mentioned are only the possible successive stages of a discussion.

The development of inference as a method of proof, by the construction of a true syllogism, is the most interesting part of these systems. The right methods of reasoning have been discussed with as much subtlety as by any of the Western logicians. A complete syllogism, in the Hindū system, consists of five members or parts (*avayava*): (1.) The proposition (*pratijnā*), (2.) the reason (*hetu* or *apadeśa*), (3.) the instance or example (*udāharana* or *nidarśana*), (4.) the application of the reason (*upanaya*), and (5.) the conclusion (*nigamana*).

Ex. (1.) This hill is fiery,
(2.) For it smokes.
(3.) Whatever smokes is fiery, as a kitchen-hearth, &c.
(4.) This hill is smoking,
(5.) Therefore it is fiery.

Or,
(1.) Sound is non-eternal,
(2.) Because it is produced.
(3.) Whatever is produced is non-eternal, as pots, &c.
(4.) Sound is produced,
(5.) Therefore it is not eternal.

Some confine the syllogism to three members, either the first three or the last: in the latter form it is the same as the syllogism of Aristotle.

The term *vyāpti* (pervasion or invariable concomitance) is used to express the connection in the major premiss of the Aristotelian syllogism. Inference is defined as the knowledge which is caused by the knowledge of *vyāpti*[1] or a knowledge "generable by a mediate judgment" (*parā-*

[1] Vyāptijnana-karanakam jnānam.

marśa).[1] "This mediate judgment is a recognition that there is in the subject of the question (*paksha*) an attribute characterised by a pervasion (or universal concomitance, *vyāpti*). In other words, the subject of the question has a property universally accompanied by something else, viz., by that which is to be proved or disproved of it by the *sādhya* or predicate of the conclusion."[2] The meaning of this term, *vyāpti*, is fully explained by *Śankara Miśra*. "It may be asked, What is this invariable concomitance? It is not merely a relation of co-extension. Nor is it the relation of totality. For if you say that invariable concomitance is the connection of the middle term with the whole of the major term, such connection does not exist in the case of smoke [for smoke does not always exist where there is fire]. Nor is it natural conjunction, for the nature of a thing is the thing's proper mode of being. . . . Nor is it the possession of a form determined by the same connection as something else; as, for instance, the being fiery is not determined by connection with smoke, for the being fiery is more extensive. We proceed, then, to state that invariable concomitance is a connection requiring no qualifying term or limitation. It is an extensiveness co-extensive with the predicate. In other words, invariable concomitance is invariable co-inherence of the predicate."[3]

The qualifying term or limitation is called *upādhi*. Fire always underlies smoke, but smoke does not always accompany fire; and the proposition that smoke accompanies fire requires a qualifying condition (*upādhi*)—that there must be moist fuel—which may not be present. An universal proposition is not therefore simply conver-

[1] Parāmarśa-janyam jnānam.

[2] Professor Gough, Calcutta Review, January 1876.

[3] Mr. Gough's translation (Indian Wisdom), p. 73.

tible, but only convertible by limitation *per accidens.* The *upādhi* is the limitation or qualifying condition which is necessary for the conversion of the proposition.

The process by which the *vyāpti* is determined is called *vyāptigraha,* and is a generalisation by experience or induction. Induction is defined as "the determination of unconditional and of conditional concomitances." The Hindū logicians are quite aware of the necessity of a sound induction for the establishment of an universal proposition. From a passage in "Muktāvalī" (p. 122) we learn that such a proposition must be proved by affirmative and negative induction, which correspond to the methods of Agreement and Difference in Mill's "Logic" (i. 454), the object being to discover a certain relation of cause and effect in the two phenomena. "The two suggestors of the relation of cause and effect are (1.) this concomitancy of affirmatives—that whenever the product exists the material cause thereof exists; and (2.) this concomitancy of negatives—that when the material cause no longer exists the product no longer exists." [1]

The system of Kanāda (the *Vaiśeshika*) is supplementary to that of Gotama, coinciding with it in the main, but differing from it in allowing only two methods of proof, perception and inference, and in its arrangement of the objects of knowledge. It is expounded in the "Vaiśeshika Sūtra, which contains about 550 aphorisms.

There are in this system six categories or predicaments (*padārtha*): (1.) things or substance; (2.) quality; (3.) action; (4.) community or genus; (5.) particularity; (6.) the co-inherence or intimate connection of constituent parts,

[1] Comm. on the Sānkhya Sutras, Professor Cowell's note to Colebrooke, i. 314.

to which later writers added a seventh, non-existence or negation (*abhāva*).

The first category, substance (*dravya*) is subdivided into nine divisions: (1.) earth (*pṛithivī*); (2.) water (*āpas*); (3.) light (*tejas*); (4.) air (*vāyu*); (5.) ether (*ākāśa*); (6.) time (*kāla*); (7.) space (*diś*); (8.) soul (*ātman*); and (9.) the internal organ, mind (*manas*). Of these, the first four and the ninth are affirmed to be formed of atoms. These atoms are round, extremely minute, invisible, incapable of division, eternal in themselves but not in their aggregate forms. They have individually a specific difference (*viśesha*). Light, for example, is formed by the aggregation of luminous atoms. Other substances are formed in a similar manner. These atoms combine by twos in an aggregate called *dwy-aṇuka*, or by threes, forming an aggregate called *trasa-reṇu*, which comes within the range of our sight, as a mote in a sunbeam. They also combine by fours, &c. They are innumerable in extent, and are perpetually united, disintegrated, and redintegrated by an unseen peculiar virtue or force (*adṛishṭa*).

What idea Kaṇāda intended to convey by the term *adṛishṭa*, the Unseen, it is not possible to say. The term *Īśwara*=God, as ruler, is not found in the *Sūtras* ascribed to him. He may mean a force or "potentiality" inherent in the atoms themselves. His disciples, however, who were affected by the teaching of Gotama, or the popular Vedānta system, explain this unseen force to be the Supreme Spirit, who is declared to be the framer of all things. They argue for the existence of a controlling Mind from the existence of effects; from the combinations of the atoms; from the support of the earth in the sky;

from traditional arts, and from the Vedas. As Kaṇāda differed from Gotama in not admitting speech or tradition as a source of knowledge, it may be doubted whether he would have admitted an argument founded on the Vedas. They appeal, however, chiefly to the evidence of design. "The earth must have had a Maker," says *Haridāsa*, "because it is an effect, like a jar."[1] This is the argument which Paley has so largely developed, now often rejected, but yet gaining assent from the common sense of mankind.

The traditional arts are those which have been handed down from father to son, which, it is argued, must have been first taught or inspired by a superintending Mind. It is implied that the inventive, creative mind of man must have been created by a power possessing like qualities, but of an infinitely higher kind. Kaṇāda certainly taught that the soul is distinct from matter. He appeals, in proof, to our feelings of desire and aversion, which are excited by a perception of the good or evil connected with certain things; affirming that this perception of good and bad results is an attribute of spirit. He combats the assertion of an objector that the soul might be diffused in matter, and not be separate from it, by asserting that the nature of the cause is always seen in the effect, and that if soul were diffused through matter, all matter would be animate.

In the second category, "quality," Kaṇāda recognised seventeen varieties in the nine substances, of which soul is one. These qualities are colour, savour, odour, tangibility, number, extension, individuality, conjunction, disjunction, priority, posteriority, intellections (*buddhayas*),

[1] Indian Wisdom, p. 88.

pleasure, pain, desire, aversion, and volition. To these his followers added the seven following: gravity, fluidity, viscidity, self-reproduction (including motion, elasticity, and memory), sound, with merit and demerit.

Light and heat are considered as only different forms of the same substance.

The direct instrument of vision is a ray of light proceeding from the pupil of the eye to the object seen. This ray of light is not ordinarily visible, as the brightness of a torch is not seen in the meridian light, but may be seen at night in the eye of a cat or other animal watching for its prey.

Ether (ākāśa) is uncompounded, infinite, and eternal. It is not atomic. It is known only by inference. It has the quality of sound, and hearing is formed by means of a portion of ether confined in the hollow of the ear and endowed with an occult virtue.

The mind (*manas*) is considered to be, as in the system of Gotama, extremely small, as an atom, and thus only one sensation is conveyed to the soul at one time. It is eternal, distinct from both soul and body, with which it is only conjoined.

Gravity is the peculiar cause of a body falling to the ground. It affects earth and water. Lightness is not a distinct quality, but only the negation of gravity.

Time is inferred from the relation of priority and subsequence, other than that of place. It is marked by associations of objects with the sun's revolutions.

Space is inferred from the relation of priority and subsequence other than that of time. It is deduced from the notion of *here* and *there*.

The third category, action (*karman*), is divided into five

kinds, upward and downward movement, contraction, dilatation, and going, or motion in general.

The fourth category, community (*sāmānya*), is the source of our notion of genus. In its highest degree it expresses only existence, a property common to all, but it usually denotes qualities common to many objects. It denotes species also, as indicating a class. These genera and species have a real, objective existence. The Bauddhas deny this, affirming that individuals only have existence, and that abstractions are false conceptions. It is the quarrel revived in the Realist and Nominalist theories of the mediæval schoolmen.

The fifth category, particularity (*viśesha*), denotes simple objects, devoid of community. These are soul, mind, time, place, the ethereal element, and also atoms in their ultimate form.

The sixth category, co-inherence or inseparable connection (*samavāya*), denotes the connection of things that in their nature must be connected so long as they exist, as yarn and the cloth of which it is formed; for so long as the yarn subsists the cloth remains.

The seventh category, subsequently added, negation or privation (*abhāva*), is of two kinds, universal and mutual. Universal negation includes three species: (1.) antecedent, a present negation of what will be at some future time, as in yarn before the production of cloth; (2.) emergent, which is destruction or cessation of an effect, as in a broken jar; (3.) absolute, implying that which never existed, as fire in a lake.

Mutual privation is essential difference, a reciprocal negation of identity, as in cloth and a jar.

The system of Kaṇāda, in its modern form at least, is

essentially a dualism; eternal atoms existing together with eternal soul, whether the latter term be confined to individual souls or includes the Supreme Soul (*Paramātman*). In every Hindū system of philosophy, Matter is supposed to be eternal, generally as a real and distinct entity in itself, except in the school of the Vedāntists, by whom it is regarded as *māyā,* the illusive manifestation of the One Supreme Brahmā, who is himself the All.

Gotama and Kaṇāda, like Kapila, could see no higher aim or blessing for mankind than a complete deliverance from pain. They agree with him in maintaining that this deliverance must be wrought out by knowledge, meaning thereby a knowledge of philosophy, and that the state to which the soul may rise by knowledge, its best and final state, is that of a tranquil unconscious passivity, in which all thought and emotion and the sense of personality have passed away for ever.

NOTES.

NOTE A.

On the Organs of the Soul in the System of Kapila.

Distichs 22, 24, 26, 34.

The Intellect (*buddhi*), the first emanation of Nature (*Prakṛiti*), is an organ or instrument of the Soul, for by it all material things are brought within the view of the Soul, which is immaterial. From it Consciousness or Mind-stuff emanates, and from Consciousness, affected by the mode of Nature called "goodness," issue the eleven organs (*indriyāni*), which are the Mind (*manas*), the five organs of sensation and the organs of action. From it also emanate the five subtle elements of matter when it is affected by the mode called "darkness," and from the subtle elements the grosser elements are evolved. The five organs of sensation are called "intellect-organs" (*buddhi-indriyāni*), and in Distich 34 they are said to be the domain of specific and non-specific elements (as Lassen translates the passage), or to concern objects specific and unspecific (as Colebrooke translates it). The meaning is obscure, and, as usual, the Hindū commentators throw no light on the darkness. Gauḍapāda assumes that by non-specific objects are meant such as are apprehended by the gods. If so, they would have no place in the system of Kapila. His meaning may probably be ascertained by noting that he regards these organs as a direct emanation from Consciousness, affected by "goodness," and therefore as being more subtle productions than even the subtle elements of what are usually called material things or gross existences. But the eye, for instance, as an organ of sight belongs to this last class. It is formed entirely of gross matter. It seems then that Kapila meant by "intellect-organs" something of a very different nature. The organ of sight is, in his theory, twofold: (1.) a subtle organisation in which the *faculty* of seeing dwells; and (2.) an instrument, the eye, which is formed of grosser elements. The faculty by which we see was connected by Kapila directly with Consciousness, and by it a sense-perception, which is defined by the *manas*, is gained. Without it the eye could no more see than in the case of a dead body. Sometimes the faculty and its instrument are united in one expression. Hence, I think, we may explain Distich 34 as meaning that the "intellect-organs" are composed of non-specific substances, *i.e.*, of the more subtle or ethereal forms of matter in the faculty of seeing, and of specific or the grosser elements in the instrument, *i.e.*, the eye. This distinction seems to have partly suggested itself to the author of the "S. Tattwa Kaumudī," for he supposes that by "non-specific" are meant such objects as are too subtle in their nature to be seen by ordinary men. Whether Kapila meant farther to say that this finer element or organisation could be known through the *buddhi* to Soul, is an inquiry that we may lay aside as having no practical importance.

If this interpretation is correct, the theory of Kapila has some resemblance to the conclusions of modern science. "Sensation proper is not purely a passive state, but implies a certain amount of mental activity. It may be described, on the psychological side, as resulting directly from the attention which the mind gives to the affections of its own organism."

"Numerous facts prove demonstrably that a certain application and exercise of mind on one side is as necessary to the existence of sensation as the occurrence of a physical impulse on the other" (Morell, Elements of Psychology, pp. 107, 108).

NOTE B.

On the Meaning of *Sat* and *Asat*.

There is a general misunderstanding of these terms as used in the philosophy of the Hindūs, especially in the system of Kapila. *Sat* is supposed to mean existence *per se*, and *asat* is therefore represented as its logical opposite, or rather contradictory; the negation of being, or non-existence. Thus Dr. Muir writes: "These ideas of entity and nonentity seem to have been familiar to the Vedic poets, and we find it thus declared (R.-V. x. 72, 2, 3), that in the beginning nonentity was the source of entity. 'In the earliest age of the gods entity sprang from nonentity; in the first age of the gods entity sprang from nonentity [*asat*].' In the Atharva-Veda (x. 7, 10) it is said that 'both nonentity and entity exist within the god Skambha;' and in v. 25 of the same hymn, 'Powerful indeed are those gods who sprang from nonentity. Men say that that nonentity is one, the highest member of Skambha.' The Taittiriya Upanishad also (p. 99) quotes a verse to the effect: 'This was at first nonentity. From that sprang entity [*sat*].'" And in a note he adds: "This phrase is also applied to Agni in R.-V. x. 5, 7, where it is said that that god, being 'a thing both *asat*, non-existent (*i.e.*, unmanifested), and *sat*, existent (*i.e.*, in a latent state or in essence), in the highest heaven, in the creation of Daksha, and in the womb of Aditi, became in a former age the first-born of our ceremonial, and is both a bull and a cow'" (Progress of the Vedic Religion, Journal A. S., 1865, p. 347). So also Professor Max Müller writes: "Some of the ancient sages, after having arrived at the idea of Avyākṛita, Undeveloped, went even beyond, and instead of the *sat* or τὸ ὄν, they postulated an *asat*, τὸ μὴ ὄν, as the beginning of all things. Thus we read in the Chāndogya Upanishad, 'And some say in the beginning there was *asat* (not being) alone, without a second; and from this *asat* might the *sat* be born'" (Sans. Literature, p. 324). There is occasionally some confusion in the minds of Hindū writers, especially the later ones, about the meaning of *sat* and *asat;* but, with Kapila and his exponents, *sat* denotes the existence of things in the manifold forms of the external world, the *Daseyn* of Hegel, the *Natura naturata* of Spinoza, and *asat* is the opposite of this, or the formless Prakṛiti, the Mind-matter from which all formal existence has sprung. *Sat* corresponds in each separate form to the "being-this" of Hegel, and Kapila argues, as the German philosopher, that "by virtue of its predicate of merely being-this, every something is a finite," and therefore it is an *effect*, because otherwise we could only conceive it as absolute being, and therefore unlimited. Soul was something different from both. So in the S'atapatha Brāhmaṇa (x. 5, 3, 1) it is said, "In the beginning this universe was, as it were, and was not, as it were. Then it was only that mind. Wherefore it has been declared by the ṛishi, 'There was then neither nonentity (*asat*) nor entity (*sat*); for mind was, as it were, neither entity nor nonentity.'" The meaning is that mind is neither the primal matter (*Prakṛiti*) (which Kapila assumed to be the source of all formal existence), nor the sum of existing things. The Vedāntists taught that this primal matter was the *śakti*, or productive energy of Brahma. So says Sankara Āchārya, "We (Vedāntists) consider that this primordial state of the world is dependent upon the Supreme Deity (Parameśwara), and not self-dependent. And this state to which we refer must of necessity be assumed, as it is essential; for without it the creative action of the Supreme Deity could not be accomplished, since if he were destitute of his *śakti*, any activity on his part would be inconceivable" (Comm. on the Brahma Sūtras, Muir's Sans. Texts, iii. 164). The full development of the Vedāntist doctrine made the external world to be only *māyā*, illusion. There is really neither *sat* nor *asat*, but the Supreme Spirit is absolutely the All. Nature is only the projection of the One, or, as Hegel thought (for he was essentially a Vedāntist), "the idea in its externality, in having fallen from itself into a without in time and space;" but this is only a manifestation of the Absolute. "The Absolute, the being-thinking [the ultimate synthesis of existence and thought, of object and subject] passes through the three periods, and manifests itself as idea in and for itself [thinking]; secondly, in its being otherwise, or in objectiveness and externality [nature]; thirdly, as the idea which from its externality has returned into itself [mind]" (Chalybäus, Hist. of Spec. Phil., Eng. ed., p. 362). As Mr. Morrell has expounded his views, and correctly, I may add, "With him God is not a *person*, but personality itself, *i.e.*, the universal personality which realises itself in every human consciousness as so many separate thoughts of one eternal mind. . . . God is with him the whole process of thought, combining in itself the objective movement as seen in Nature, with the subjective as seen in logic, and fully realising itself only in the universal spirit of humanity" (Mod. Phil., ii. 189). Pure Vedāntism! though Hegel, if he were alive, would protest against such a statement. But Kapila was not a Vedāntist. With him the aggregate of existing things and each separate existence (*sat*), and the formless Prakṛiti from which they issued (*asat*), were objectively real and eternally distinct from Soul, though both Soul and Prakṛiti are eternal and uncaused.

Dr. Muir, however, refers to the commentators on the Rig-Veda who explain *asat* as meaning "an undeveloped state," and adds that if we accept this statement there will be no contradiction. *Asat* does not mean simply an undeveloped state, but the state of pure or formless existence of the primal substance from which all forms have sprung. It is clear, however, that if *asat* means an undeveloped state, then *sat* must mean, not the essence of anything, but a developed state, the development of the existing world, as Kapila uses it. The writer of the Vedic hymn (R.-V. x. 57) meant to say that Agni was *asat*, but became *sat* in the birth (*janman*) of Daksha and in the womb of Aditi. It is clear, also, that Kapila, in this part of his system, incorporated an older theory, in which *asat* denoted at least the undeveloped state from which existing things have been developed. *Sat* was the whole of existent things. In Rig-Veda, i. 96, 7, Agni is called *satas gōpa*, the guardian of that which has a present being. There is also the germ of another part of his system in a hymn of this Veda (x. 129): "There was then neither *asat* nor *sat*." There was only the one Supreme Spirit dwelling in self-existence. "Desire, then, in the beginning (*ágrē*) arose in It, which was the earliest germ of mind, and wise men have beheld in their heart, not being ignorant, that this is the bond between *asat* and *sat*." In the system of Kapila it is an unconscious impulse on the part of Prakṛiti, or instinctive desire to set the soul free from matter which causes the emanation of Prakṛiti into the manifold forms of developed life (*sat*). This latter was, in Kapila's view, an effect, because developed, and implying therefore a developing cause.

NOTE C.

ON THE CONNECTION OF THE SĀNKHYA SYSTEM WITH THE PHILOSOPHY OF SPINOZA.

The teaching of Spinoza has been unjustly described as a pure Atheism or as a system based on Materialism. This error has apparently arisen from his use of the word "substantia," which he is supposed to use to denote mere matter or gross body, in opposition to mind or spirit. He uses it, however, to denote absolute or infinite Being with infinite attributes, manifesting itself by modes or accidents (affectiones) in the manifold forms of the universe, and to this absolute substance or Being he gives the name of God. To God he sometimes gives the name of Nature, as Kapila called his primal substance Prakṛiti. "Infinitum ens, quod Deum sive naturam, appellamus, eadem, qua existit, necessitate agit" (Eth. iv.). But he made a distinction between God as the source of formal existence and these existences themselves, calling the one *Natura naturans* and the other *Natura naturata.* God is the cause of all things, not of their existence merely, but of their essence, and this not transiently but immanently. God is the only substance, whether as *Natura naturans* or *Natura naturata.* Whatever is, is in God, and without God nothing can be conceived, for as the Infinite Substance he is the source of all things, and they are contained in Him. Thus, as others who have attempted to solve the mysterious problem of the relation of the Infinite to the Finite, he forms only a kind of Pantheism. It has been said that "Spinoza does not confound God with the material universe," but this is, in his system, a part of God: "Natura naturans et natura naturata in identitate Deus est." God has, indeed, two attributes, thought and expansion. "Cogitatio attributum Dei est, sive Deus est res cogitans. Extensio attributum Dei est, sive Deus est res extensa" (Eth. 2). But here are not two distinct entities. God is the All. Extension is visible thought and thought is invisible extension, but He is the living whole. "Res particulares nihil sunt nisi Dei attributorum affectiones, sive modi, quibus Dei attributa certo et de terminato modo exprimuntur" (Eth. i.). God, however, is not corporeal. The universe is only a manifestation of his being. Body is only a mode of his attribute of extension, a passing form of his existence. All formal existence changes and dies; it is but a visible aspect of him who is unchangeable and eternal. He, the Infinite, exists in himself, and that which is finite exists in another, and cannot therefore be a representation of his nature. As Cousin has interpreted the idea: the universe is "the Deity passing into activity, but not exhausted by the act" (Cours de Phil. Intro.).

In his psychology Spinoza taught that the mind does not know itself, except so far as it receives ideas of sensation by the bodily organs; but these perceptions, which are primarily confused, become clear by the action of the mind in internal reflection. It is not, however, free in its action. It is determined by a cause, which is itself determined *ad infinitum* by some other cause. All things issue and are carried on by an eternal necessity. Even God does not act for some voluntary purpose, for this would indicate desire. He acts only from the necessity of his nature. As there is no free will and no really free action, for man is but a part of the general order whose laws cannot be disturbed, there is no absolute goodness or its opposite, and men have invented the names of goodness or virtue to denote such actions as tend to their benefit. God is really the cause of all things, even of our thoughts; of the latter by his attribute of thought, and of outward actions by his attribute of extension. Men attribute their actions to the determination of the mind, not knowing, in their ignorance, that the mind cannot think till it is impelled by the bodily organs, and our volitions are only our appetites which are connected with the body.

Spinoza taught that truth, *i.e.*, the just correlation of idea and fact, might be obtained. Ideas are obtained (1.) by the action of the bodily senses; (2.) in their generic form by imagination, *i.e.*, the remembrance of sensational ideas, which are classified by words; (3.) by the logical faculty or reason; and (4.) by intuition, as Schelling afterwards taught. Error arises from the confused and imperfect results of the first source of knowledge. There is no faculty of thought or of desire, as distinguished from the act, and both mind and body "are but one thing considered under different attributes." There is ultimately an identity, as in the system of Hegel, of subject and object, and this oneness is in God. It is not made evident how Spinoza reconciled the apparently opposite ideas of the spirituality of the Divine nature and the real existence of material forms. If the latter are only his visible aspect, a realisation of himself in the material world, and particular things are only modes of his attribute of extension, we have a near approach to the Vedāntist doctrine of *māyā* (illusion), which represents the whole of formal, material existence to be only an illusive manifestation of the One Supreme Spirit, who is himself the All.

It will be unnecessary to say to those who have read the "Sānkhya Kārikā" that the system of Kapila is not the same as that of Spinoza; but the latter, as an exposition of God and Nature, has a close resemblance to the theistic form of the Sankhya as set forth by Patanjali, and especially to this form of it as represented in the "Bhagavad Gītā." In that work the One Supreme Being has a dual nature, a higher which is spiritual, and a lower which answers to the Prakṛiti of Kapila, and corresponds to the attributes of God—thought and expansion—in the system of Spinoza. The world of existing things is a manifestation of the Supreme Spirit in this lower attribute, coming forth at the will of the spiritual nature and again at the end of an age called a *kalpa*, dissolving into his all-containing self. All individual or formal existence is but the modal form in which the one spiritual essence makes itself manifest. All things issue from this source and are contained in it. As the ether pervades and encompasses all things, so the One pervades and encompasses all. Spinoza might have employed the language of the "Bhagavad Gītā," and the author of this work might have taught, in the words of Spinoza, "Deum esse non tantum causam, ut res incipiant existere, sed etiam, ut in existendo perseverent; sive (ut termino scholastico utar), Deum esse causam essendi rerum" (Eth. i.). Both taught that the universe was an evolution, but not such an evolution as Darwin has endeavoured to prove—from the lowest point of being to its highest state—but from the one highest or sole being to its lowest depths, there being a gradation from *buddhi* (intellect) down to inanimate matter. The one, in this gradation, ends where the other begins. The Hindū and the German philosopher moved, in other respects, in precisely the same lines of thought. Both taught that the mind or the soul knows itself only by the action of the ideas of sensation or sense-perceptions that originate in the bodily organs. There is no absolute self-consciousness.

In another conclusion the two systems agree. The fatalism which Spinoza asserted, though supported by a more imposing array of argument and more absolute in its kind, is maintained by his Hindū predecessor. According to the latter, the universe is only a vast machine, which is caused to revolve by the action of the One Being, in whom all existence is contained. All things are but the agents of his power; and though virtue and vice have an essential difference from each other, yet a fatal necessity destroys, in fact, the barriers that, in the conscience of mankind, are placed between good and evil. Conscience has no part in either system. Man seeks only his own advantage, though in the system of Patañjali the highest good is obtained by an absorption into the divine essence by *yoga* (lit. union), the blending of the human with the divine, even in this life, by the force of constant meditation. The Deity has no concern with human actions, whether good or bad. The perfect man has no sympathy with his fellows. He lives in a state of complete isolation, in which all necessity for action and all sense of duty are entirely lost. The system of Spinoza leads to the same selfish exclusiveness; for if men ought to seek only what is profitable or agreeable to them, or rather, must do so from the very necessity of their nature, there is no possibility of self-sacrifice or the abandonment of a personal gain for the benefit of others, either in their personal or national capacity. There is virtually no law, or no law but that of an unchangeable necessity, and all rightfulness and the sense of right or wrong are absolutely destroyed.

NOTE D.

ON THE CONNECTION OF THE SYSTEM OF KAPILA WITH THAT OF SCHOPENHAUER AND VON HARTMANN.

The philosophical system of Spinoza has many points in common with the theory of Patanjali, but the teaching of Kapila is more closely allied with the latest philosophy of Germany, as set forth by Schopenhauer and Von Hartmann, in "Die Welt als Wille und Vorstellung" ("The World as Will and Idea") of the first, and the "Philosophie des Unbewussten" ("Philosophy of the Unconscious") of the latter. If we leave out of view Hartmann's poetical illustrations of his subject, by which he gives an unnatural brightness to a gloomy system, we shall find only a "philosophy of despair," an inarticulate cry, a wail of lamentation in which there is no hope. There is absolutely none for man in his present conscious life. Its pleasures are chiefly a mere absence of pain, and pain meets us at every step. Riches bring with them many cares, together with much toil; and labour—a thoroughly Hindū sentiment—is itself an evil. Love brings upon us embarrassments and disappointment; it requires immense sacrifices; it causes more pain than pleasure; it is an "evil," or at best an "illusion." Nor can sympathy, as some falsely suppose, bring pleasure to the man who offers it: it is only another form of pain. Ambition is a mere delusion, a vain striving—which is itself an evil—for that which will only mock us if attained, and cause bitter sorrow if, as the course of affairs usually runs, we are left to pine in solitude for the unattained object of our dreams.

The pleasures of science and art are rarely obtained, and if they are won, they are only gained by much toil and continual sacrifice. The end, if gained, is not a compensation for the substantial evils of the method of our success; and our intellectual elevation makes us only more sensitive of pain. A dog or an ox is happier, or rather less miserable, than man, for it has a lower sensibility in proportion as it has a duller intellect. Hope, indeed, remains, and might give a real enjoyment, but we have learned by experience that our hopes are deceptive: they only make our miserable state more sad and despairing from the false light which they throw around us for a while, leaving us, in their departure, immersed in a deeper darkness and at a lower depth. "Human life," says Schopenhauer, "oscillates between pain and ennui, which two states are indeed the ultimate elements of life." Hartmann says of love that "the sorrow of disappointment and the bitterness of betrayal continue infinitely longer than the happiness of the illusion." Kapila taught, also, that our present life is occupied and made miserable by pain, which comes upon mankind from three different sources. In the Sūtras attributed to him it is declared that "the complete destruction of pain is the highest object of man" (i. 1). Pain is, therefore, the chief evil, if not, as Jeremy Bentham maintained, the only evil in the world, and the sole purpose of the wise is to learn how it may be put away for ever. Virtue and vice are determined only by the tendency of actions to produce pleasure or pain. There is no absolute or moral difference; in fact, morality may be discarded from our thoughts: the soul, in the system of Kapila—for he believed in the existence of souls—having no direct connection with virtue or vice, which are only material conditions. To strive for inward purity, or to contend for a noble purpose in our own lives or for the benefit of others, was not indeed to him, as to some modern philosophers, a work of folly or delusion, but it was not held to be man's highest or most necessary purpose. This is found only in the attainment of the knowledge by which the soul may be freed from all contact with matter, that by such means pain may be destroyed. There is no greatness in the suffering of pain, no moral elevation in sharing the pains or the sorrows of others. Philosophy began, as it ends, by seeking only to obtain a painless, untroubled life.

If now the question be put, How was this state of misery produced? the answer in the two systems is substantially the same. The nature of the kosmos is explained in different terms, but in each the sum of existent things has been developed from a primary unconscious substance or force, which Schopenhauer describes as Will, of which the world is an objective manifestation, and which Hartmann calls "the Unconscious." This is the all-containing principal or primal source of all formal existence, the ὕλη of the Greeks. "The Unconscious is the ultimate principle of all existence; it enters into all organic forces, into all our bodily movements and our mental processes; it guides man through all the stages of his life, and without man's knowledge it directs his steps so as to realise its plans; it lies at the root and forms the essence of both matter and spirit; they are therefore identical, and only different aspects of the self-same substance."[1] If we substitute mind as the formative power or faculty of ideas for spirit, this would serve for a description of the Prakṛiti of Kapila. This is the universal primordial monad, from which have emanated all the different states of mind and matter. It enfolds and animates all things, and all things will be finally absorbed and lost in it. In its primary state it was in a condition of equilibrium, and there was no development of formal existence while it continued in that state. How then was this passive state brought to an end and the beginning of the existing kosmos produced? The answer of Kapila is that the proximity of Prakṛiti (Nature) to Soul gave rise to an unconscious movement of Nature's constitutent elements, that by their consequent unfolding into the forms of material life the Soul might know the existence of matter and be subsequently free from all contact with it. The Soul thus knows itself and gains its natural state of isolation. All existing things have been formed for this purpose. So says Hegel: "Everything in heaven and earth aims only at this—that the soul may know itself, may make itself its object, and close together with itself." The doctrine of Schopenhauer is that everything, physical or mental, is an emanation of that mysterious force called Will, which has thus changed itself from subject to object, and that this includes all things and all beings, so that the idea of self or individuality is an illusion. Hartmann represents the Unconscious as the unity of Will and Idea, the latter being the object which the Will unconsciously

[1] See an able article on the "Philosophy of Pessimism" in the "Westminster Review," January 1876.

seeks to realise. The Idea has no separate existence *per se*, and here we come very near the Vedāntist doctrine of *māyā* (illusion). Schopenhauer, however, says that "absence of end belongs to the nature of Will *per se*, which is an endless striving" (Die Welt als Wille, &c.). From neither do we learn how the world of existent things came to be developed from this unknown power called Will, but the German philosophers agree with Kapila in maintaining that the primary essence or substance was unconscious, and that the conscious life has been developed from it. Hartmann speaks of the Unconscious as being properly that which is above consciousness (*das Ueberbewusste*), and that an individual consciousness is a limitation and defect. Its birth is explained in language which is probably as strange as any that the science of mental physiology has ever known : "Before the rise of consciousness, mind can, in its own nature, have no other presentations and ideas than those which are called into being through Will and form its content. Suddenly organised matter breaks in upon this peace of the Unconscious with itself"—as in the system of Kapila the external world is presented to the soul by *Buddhi* (Intellect)—"and impresses on the astonished individual mind, in the necessary reaction of the sensation, a conception which falls upon it as it were from heaven, because it finds within itself no Will for this idea; for the first time the content of intuition is given it from outside" (Phil. d. Unb., p. 394). Consciousness is, therefore, the surprise of the unconscious Will in an individual mind at the presence of an idea which the senses present.

Kapila has not ventured upon such flights of fancy, but he preceded Schopenhauer and Hartmann in asserting that the misery of our present state is due to the fact of our conscious life, for this has arisen from material developments which cause pain, and this can be put away only when consciousness has ceased to exist. When the soul has gained a complete isolation, then all conscious life is absorbed into the unconscious Prakṛiti. Freedom from pain can only be obtained by the destruction of this conscious life, and the aim of the wise is to obtain by knowledge the primitive state of unconsciousness. Schopenhauer and Hartmann teach the same doctrine. There is no remedy for the misery of the world in anything that belongs to our present life. It has its root in consciousness, which is found in every kind of formal existence, even the lowest, but has its highest development in man, and hence he is supremely wretched. But the remedy for the evil is not suicide: this affects only the individual; it cannot benefit the race. "The basis of all man's being is want, defect, and pain. Since he is the most complete objective form of will, he is by that same fact the most defective of all beings. His life is only a continual struggle for existence, with the certainty of being beaten" (Die Welt als Wille). How, then, is the world to be delivered from this state of wretchedness? The answer is: (1.) By a knowledge of the fact that the world in its present form is wholly and unalterably bad. This answers to Kapila's statement that our deliverance from pain can only be gained by knowledge. (2.) By the abandonment of desire, the renunciation of will, the absolute surrender of personal existence, that all things may be absorbed into the unconscious. Thus the whole of present formal existence will pass away for ever. The world, as it now is, was an irrational development of will. "As man becomes penetrated with the idea of the misery of existence, and the feeling gains strength through heredity; as people become more capable of co-operation, the greater portion of the active spirit in the world will adopt the resolution to destroy the act of will, and the world will have vanished into nothingness. The unconscious will return to that passive state of pure self-satisfied intelligence from which it never should have passed; and the possibility of another world, with all the miseries of this, will be for ever exhausted and exterminated" (West. Rev., p. 159). In the system of Kapila this state of unconsciousness, of calm and eternal repose, is gained by the soul when absolutely freed from contact with matter, and the whole of formal or developed existence will be absorbed into the formless, unconscious Prakṛiti. Hartmann, too, asserts a true *Nirvāṇa*, the extinction of all conscious personal life as the final goal which the wise will seek to obtain. The Hindū and the German philosopher alike maintain that there is no hope for the world by any process of amendment. The labours of statesmen and philanthropists are in vain. The only sufficient and abiding cure of its woes is the annihilation of all individual life. The last act of the great drama, which we are to expect eagerly, ends in the universal destruction of the present order, and the world, with all its miseries, will pass away for ever. The German philosopher has a more Vedāntist leaning than Kapila. The unconscious that will reabsorb all existence in itself bears a close resemblance to the supreme Brahma, who is the efficient and material cause of all created things, or rather they are, as the Vedāntists say, himself in certain deceptive forms, which shall finally disappear, and all life, as at the beginning, shall be absorbed and contained in him. M. Renan anticipates a similar result as the conclusion of the existing world. "We imagine a state of the world in which everything would end alike in a single conscious centre in which the universe would be reduced to a single existence, in which the idea of a personal monotheism would be a truth. A Being omniscient and omnipotent might be the last term of the deific evolution, whether we conceive him as rejoicing in all (all also rejoicing in him), according to the dream of the Christian mysticism, or as an individuality attaining to a supreme force, or as the resultant of tens of thousands of beings, as the harmony, the total voice of the universe. The universe would be thus consummated in a single organised being, in whose infinitude would be resumed millions of millions of lives, past and present, at the same time." This sole Being is further described in language which, from its united grandeur and grotesqueness, might have been written in the East, and will remind the Sanskrit scholar of the description of the Supreme Being in the eleventh chapter of the Bhagavad Gītā: "Only a small part of matter is now organised, and that which is organised is organised feebly; but we may admit an age in which all matter may be organised, in which thousands of suns joined together would serve to form a single being, sentient, rejoicing, absorbing by his burning throat a river of pleasure which would flow from him in a torrent of life. This living universe would present the two poles which every nervous mass presents, the pole which feels and the pole which enjoys. Now, the universe thinks and rejoices by millions of individuals. One day a colossal mouth would give a sense of the infinite (*savourerait l'infini*), an ocean of intoxicating delight (*un ocean d'ivresse*) would flow into it; an inexhaustible emission of life, knowing neither repose nor fatigue, would spring up throughout eternity. To coagulate this divine mass the earth will probably have been taken and spoiled as a clod that one crushes without care of the ant or the worm which conceals itself there."[1] Is this philosophy or a dream? Kapila and Hartmann had substantially the same theory, but the exercise of their imagination was less bold and vivid than that of the Frenchman. But, however expressed, whether in the obscure brevity of Īśwara Kṛishṇa, or in the subtle but flowing arguments and illustrations of Hartmann, or the imaginative flights of Renan, the theory is substantially the same. All existent things have issued from the One; this emanation into separate and conscious forms of being has been the cause of unnumbered woes; and this state of misery can

[1] Dialogues Philosophiques, trois. dial. (Rèves), pp. 125-128.

only be put away by the absorption of all personal, conscious life in its primal source. The oldest and the latest system of philosophy, though severed in time by more than two thousand years, speak with the same voice; but they give no hope to man, for his highest ambition or his only refuge from misery lies in his personality being destroyed for ever.

THE END.

PRINTED BY BALLANTYNE, HANSON AND CO.
EDINBURGH AND LONDON.